AMERICAN PUBLIC UNIVERSITY SYSTEM

Charles

THE DEVELOPMENT OF   RIAN
LAW: FROM THE EMAN   . THE
UNITED STATES TO THE GENEVA CONVENTIONS

A thesis submitted in partial fulfillment of the

requirements for the degree of

MASTER OF ARTS

in

ANCIENT AND CLASSICAL HISTORY

by

Jonathan Halperin Kantor

Department Approval Date:
TBD

The author hereby grants the American Public University System
the right to display these contents for educational purposes.

The author assumes total responsibility for meeting the requirements set by United States Copyright Law for the inclusion of any materials that are not the author's creation or in the public domain.

© 2015 by Jonathan H. Kantor

All rights reserved.

ABSTRACT OF THE THESIS

THE DEVELOPMENT OF INTERNATIONAL HUMANITARIAN LAW: FROM THE EMANCIPATION OF THE SLAVES IN THE UNITED STATES TO THE GENEVA CONVENTIONS

By:

Jonathan Halperin Kantor

American Public University System,
14 June, 2015

Charles Town, West Virginia

Professor Mark Bowles, Thesis Professor

The International Committee of the Red Cross was founded in 1863 due, in large part, to the horrors of battlefield medicine in the ongoing conflict of the Austro-Sardinian War. Similarly, in America and due to the nature of battlefield medicine and the care of enemy combatants in internment camps like Andersonville and Camp Douglas as well as others all over the Confederate and United States of America, it became apparent that changes needed to be made to ensure the humane treatment of the people fighting in that bloody conflict. Because of men like Henri Dunant who witnessed the horrors of war at the Battle of Solferino in 1859, a call was made for the establishment of an international treaty to protect the humanity of soldiers in conflict. Though America was far away and well outside of the European matters of war, members came to Geneva to attend the first Geneva Convention for the Amelioration of the Condition of the Wounded and Sick in Armed Forces in the Field. The first step in making this happen began when Abraham Lincoln sought a legal means of freeing the slaves in America. To do this, he pushed for a code of the laws of war to justify his actions. As a result, the Lieber Code was drafted, which had several unforeseen consequences; the most significant of these being the creation of international laws and treaties that have helped countless millions survive the suffering atrocities of more than 150 years of warfare.

CONTENTS

CHAPTER I: INTRODUCTION

CHAPTER II: LITERATURE REVIEW

CHAPTER III: JEAN-HENRI DUNANT & THE BATTLE OF SOLFE-
RINO

CHAPTER IV: THE INTERNATIONAL COMMITTEE OF THE RED
CROSS

CHAPTER V: THE LIEBER CODE & THE PROBLEM OF EMANCIPA-
TION

CHAPTER VI: PAROLE, FURLOUGHS, AND EXCHANGES

CHAPTER VII: UNION ARMY PRISONER OF WAR CAMPS

CHAPTER VIII: CONFEDERATE ARMY PRISONER OF WAR CAMPS

CHAPTER IX: WIRZ AND THE HUMANITARIAN CRISIS IN ANDER-
SONVILLE

CHAPTER X: GENEVA CONVENTIONS & INTERNATIONAL CRIM-
INAL COURT

CHAPTER XI: CONCLUSION

APPENDIX A: THE FIRST GENVA CONVENTION

APPENDIX B: SELECTIONS FROM THE LIEBER CODE

BIBLIOGRAPHY

  Primary Sources

  Secondary Sources

FIGURES

Figure 1: After the Battle of Solferino
Figure 2: Harper's Weekly Political Cartoon
Figure 3: The Fort Pillow Massacre
Figure 4: Five largest Northern POW Camps during the Civil War by mortality rates
Figure 5: Men Enlisted at Camp Douglas
Figure 6: Camp Douglas Memorial in Chicago
Figure 7: Map of All Camps.
Figure 8: Calvin Bates
Figure 9: Andersonville
Figure 10: Starved Prisoner..
Figure 11: The Hanging of CPT. Wirz
Figure 12: Switzerland Flag – Red Cross Symbol
Figure 13: Rome Statute of the International Criminal Court

INTRODUCTION

International law can be traced back to the customs of the ancient Greek poleis as well as the Roman standards for international relations between Roman citizens and residents of other states.[1] Modern international law finds some root in the ancient practices, but was principally developed out of Renaissance Europe as various nation-states established their sovereignty and were forced to deal diplomatically with one another. Prior to the first Geneva Convention held on the 22nd of August 1864, international law was mostly concerned with matters of trade and sovereign recognition. While there was a general understanding of the need to maintain a prisoner of war's human rights for use in trade, there was little done to establish a basic principal of human rights for those captured and/or injured in warfare.

As early as the eighteenth century, informal agreements were made on the field of battle to recognize the need for hospitals to remain sacred and off limits from attack. Philanthropist Mabel T. Boardman describes an instance in which this took place when during the eighteenth century, commanders would meet in the field and come to various agreements as to the nature of what they called sacred asylums; locations that would be marked and easily identified where each side could establish field hospitals without fear of them falling to enemy action. During a conflict between the French and Austrian forces, the French surgeon-general named Percy, first brought up the suggestion of these sacred asylums and it was dependent upon the local commanders to agree on such matters, which they often did. As such, "the armies also were to favor and protect mutually the service of the hospitals in the countries that they occupied. The soldiers when recovered were to be sent back to their respective armies, with escort and safeguard."[2] While these agreements were important and beneficial for the troops on the battlefield, they were not established as law.

Even with rare agreements such as the type mentioned above, they came infrequently and only applied to the conflict at hand, and between the commanders who made the agreements. In the United States, General George Washington mandated that all captured enemy soldiers would not be denied quarter, and denied his troops any injury against the enemy. Washington wrote to Colonel Benedict Arnold on the 14th of September, 1775 his thoughts on torture of captured prisoners by saying that any American soldier who would injure any prisoner should be punished as appropriate based on the crime itself. Washington did not limit this to death and instead, indicated that the punishment should not be disproportional to the crime so that no opposing force or those who would judge their actions later would consider the newly-formed United States Army a disgrace, deserving of shame and ruin upon the soldiers and their country.[3]

Washington's views on prisoner care were revolutionary, especially considering that the British and Hessian troops treated the captured Americans as traitors who were seen as unlawful combatants and were often executed upon capture. Unfortunately, Washington's views on torture and prisoner care would not remain a law of the newly established United States of America and it would be almost a century before any such laws would be realized anywhere in the world. The first of these recognized and formal declarations of law pertaining to humanitarian care and the laws of war would be written in 1862 under the direction of President Lincoln in what has become known as the Lieber Code.

President Lincoln required a means of addressing southern concerns of a servile insurrection so that he could move forward with his plans to emancipate the slaves in newly-captured territories. In order to do this, he first needed to justify taking those freed slaves and putting them into Union Army uniforms. Lincoln decided to look towards a legal justification in what would become the Lieber Code, or General Order Number 100. The Lieber Code was the first set of rules regarding the law of war that helped the United States Army deal with the conduct of warfare during the American Civil War. The Code was the first in a long line of documents that would bring about humanitarian changes, but it also had some unforeseen consequences. Because the Lieber Code would direct that all soldiers who were captured in uniform, regardless of race, were to be considered prisoners of war and guaranteed the rights normally agreed-upon pertaining to their care, the inadvertent result would be an increase in the population of prisoner of war camps. This was due to the Confederate refusal to accept the equivalency of black and white soldiers such that neither side would agree to continue prisoner transfers between nations. This inadvertently led to a massive influx in the population of prisoners all over both the north and the south. Because of this, the United States would later come to the conclusion that a more realized code of laws on the conduct of armies during a time of war were needed. This was the main reason that the United States became involved in international humanitarian law.

It was not until warfare came to Europe in 1859 that someone took note of the horrors of conflict and came to the conclusion that some form of international treaty or law needed to be made in order to ensure the basic humanity of injured or captured soldiers. A Swiss social activist named Jean-Henri Dunant visited the wounded men following the Battle of Solferino in 1859 and was so moved by what he saw, he published a memoir of the battle and made it his life's work to create a relief agency capable of supporting humanitarian aid during war as well as establishing a treaty to enact that organization's neutrality within a designated war zone.[4] His work would culminate in the International

Association of the Red Cross and the first Geneva Convention. "This battle was also the grounds on which the international community of States has developed and adopted instruments of International Humanitarian Law, the international law rules relevant in times of armed conflict."[5] It was through the Red Cross and America's ongoing conflict that The United States was brought into the interests of European warfare.

When the International Committee of the Red Cross first began in 1863, it established the basis for humanitarian recognition and aid for the wounded and dying men in the field of combat. Additionally, it mandated rules for the recognition, safety, and noncombatant status of field medics, nurses, and doctors as well as locations such as hospitals and casualty tents. It was during this time that the United States was immersed in a conflict of its own, the American Civil War. Since 1861, the Confederate States and United States of America were locked in a struggle to remain united or to separate them into two distinct nations. The casualties were terrible on both sides and each had more wounded than they could handle. Each side claimed thousands of prisoners of war whom they would eventually house at any of several temporary and permanent prisons. Two of the most significant from the Civil War were Andersonville, Georgia and Camp Douglas, Illinois. The significance of each of these camps was not necessarily their size, though Andersonville was the largest, but the atrocities committed at each. Unlike modern prisons, these were more akin to concentration camps where the inmates were left to fend for themselves with no clothing, food, or medicine provided. In many cases, men died from exposure, dehydration, and preventable diseases such as scurvy and dysentery. The nature of these camps has been written about extensively over the previous 150 years with a great deal of attention placed on the treatment of prisoners. Many theories have been posited that suggest the lack of care given to prisoners was a result of limited resources, apathy, and even cruelty in some cases. Regardless of the reasons for the terrible state of the camps, their existence required action towards the end of the conflict. It was due to the nature of those camps as well as a need to secure the safety of medics in the field that the United States recognized a need for change and due to the aid of people like Clara Barton and Henry Dunant, America became involved in what would become one of the most important international treaties dealing with humanitarian law, The First Geneva Convention, for the Amelioration of the Condition of the Wounded in Armies in the Field.[6]

The United States was represented by two people who were granted leave by Congress at the invitation of the Geneva Society of Public Unity, George C. Fogg, the United States Minister to Switzerland, and Charles S. P. Bowles, the European agent of the Sanitary Commission.[7] They were granted permission to attend the meeting informally by the Secretary of State, William Henry Seward, who wrote in his letter of authorization, that the object of the convention was both laudable and important so there was no foreseeable objection to an informal attendance wherein the attendees could make or receive any suggestions considered humane that might lend support to the proceedings. He further stated that "It is hardly necessary to add that your presence at the congress would be improper if any of the insurgent emissaries of the United States in Europe should be permitted to take part in its proceedings."[8]

There were many advancements in battlefield medicine during the American Civil War that helped to save soldiers' lives in a way that had previously been impossible. Due to the ability to conduct somewhat sanitary surgeries in the field, many wounded men would survive otherwise fatal injuries that cost them the loss of an appendage or some other devastating injury. Even with these advances, limitations on ability and recognition of medical personnel to do their work unmolested by the enemy remained a constant problem. These issues were prevalent in the minds of the men attending the First Geneva Convention and coupled with the ongoing problems of prisoner care in both the Union and Confederacy, the United States was able to capture the humanitarian intent from the Convention, though it wouldn't become a signatory for a number of years after the conflict.

The Convention of 1864 was only the first of four that would establish the basis for humanitarian treatment of wounded and captured personnel. The treaty would be ratified in 1906 and again in 1949 following the Second World War. Each convention would clarify the previous articles and add new ones to ensure there was no future misunderstanding about how captured soldiers, and even civilians should be treated during and after a conflict. The later Conventions even outlined the appropriate use of force and the limitations of weapon and ammunition modification to inflict additional injury beyond the need of conventional warfare. Even though The United States was first an informal participant in the First Geneva Convention, it took a leading role in the following Conventions and established itself as a world power, often maintaining adherence to the Articles of the Geneva Conventions.

The treatment of prisoners of war during the American Civil War was paramount in bringing the United States to the international table dealing with humanitarian law. Because of the Lieber Code and its institution, the United States was able to both set the example for what needed to be done, but also the dangers of what might happen when such a law was used regardless of its original intent. Such actions would later bring the United States to Geneva to take part in the First and subsequent Geneva conventions. Ultimately, it was due to a series of unrelated events that would bring about the changes necessary for the creation of both the International Red Cross and the Geneva Conventions. The Battle of Solferino coupled with the need for emancipation of the slaves and the drafting of both the Lieber Code and President Jefferson Davis' General Order no., 111, which led to the halting of prisoner exchanges. This eventually led to the overcrowding and humanitarian crisis that befell the Union and Confederate prisoner of war camps and finally brought the United States to Geneva to participate in the creation of international humanitarian law. The thesis will analyze the following points: battlefield medicine during the American Civil War was hindered by a lack of enemy recognition leading to numerous deaths and capture of personnel; the need to justify both the freeing of southern slaves and the enlistment of those men as well as free blacks in the north was necessary for emancipation to continue given a southern fear of servile insurrection; the Lieber Code was the first step in recognizing a formal need to govern the care and treatment of wounded men in battle, though it ultimately led to an opposing General Order by President Davis that brought about the cessation of prisoner exchanges; the International Committee of the Red Cross was instrumental in bringing the United States to Geneva years before an American chapter was created; that the men who were captured and interned in the camps at Andersonville and Douglas were treated inhumanely such that it became necessary for the United States to recognize this fact and learn from their mistakes by accepting the articles of the Geneva Conventions. Because of the harsh treatment of captured Prisoners of War in camps like Andersonville and Douglas, the United States recognized the need for a diplomatic solution and found it in the first Geneva Convention of 1864. Though it wouldn't be ratified until 1882 due to the fractured nature of the American Civil War, America's involvement in the proceedings began the process by which the United States entered into international governance of human rights and the laws of war. Americans were far separated from the various conflicts of Europe, but were so engulfed in their own war filled with horrors of their own medicine and prisoner of war treatment that the United States was a necessary participant in the First and subsequent Geneva Conventions.

LITERATURE REVIEW

The origin of the International Committee of the Red Cross and the Geneva Conventions have been written about extensively since 1863 when the organization was founded. Primary sources from the period have survived to help future generations better understand the development of such an important event in human history. Additionally, much has been written about the American Civil War and the atrocities in both Andersonville and Camp Douglas as well as many other Civil War prisons. In addition to biographies of the people involved and recovered documents written at the time, there is a plethora of information regarding both the Civil War and the Geneva Conventions, yet with so much written about these events, there has been only a small amount of work done to explain exactly why the United States became involved in an international treaty oriented towards the proper treatment of aid workers, the injured, and prisoners of war during what would become the bloodiest conflict in United States history. One of the main reasons that the United States became interested in such a treaty or in any type of law governing the treatment of prisoners of war began with Abraham Lincoln's desire to both free the slaves and enlist them into military service in the war against the Confederacy.

While scholars such as Angela Bennett have written detailed accounts of the formation of the Red Cross and the Geneva Convention in her book, *The Geneva Convention: The Hidden Origins of the Red Cross*, which covers the impetus of Henri Dunant's desire for change in battlefield medicine after his visit at the Battle of Solferino, there is nothing to link the United States into that action. This isn't due to a lack of research or understanding of the subject; the United States wasn't involved either directly or indirectly in the very beginning of the formation of the Red Cross. While that is true, it remains an important aspect of the history of such an organization to understand how a nation like the United States did become involved since it became such a force for change on the subject of international humanitarian law in the following century. My goal in this thesis will be to uncover exactly how the United States first became involved in its own advances in humanitarian law as well as how it eventually became a significant partner in international affairs concerned with the same.

Dunant himself accounted for his time in Italy following the Battle in his own book, though Bennett does an incredible job at summarizing the entirety of that work into a concise chapter that begins with his desire to meet with Napoleon III regarding an appeal for water usage rights for his property in Algeria and ends with his return from Italy and the new direction his life would take.[9] In the following chapter, Bennett discovers in detail the impact Dunant's book would have on Moynier and his associates in Geneva, which led to the Geneva Convention and creation of the Red Cross. The book continues with great detail analysis of the earliest years of the Red Cross and the men and women who took part in its inception. What is lacking is an analysis of the involvement of the United States. United States involvement in the First Geneva Convention was largely limited to attendance since it would be years before ratification in the States, but it was that first meeting in Geneva that began the process by which the United States of America would eventually come to take part in the larger role of International politics and humanitarian issues in subsequent campaigns that brought about the first and second World Wars. This involvement first began with the emancipation of slavery in the United States and followed with the introduction of the Lieber Code, which came to influence the proceedings and discussions that took place at the First Geneva Convention in 1864.

Other books written by, on behalf of, and about the Red

Cross all contain a similar depiction of the events that led to the creation of the organization. There is a consensus amongst historians that the organization would never have existed had it not been for the events at Solferino and the meetings held in Geneva by Moynier. Subsequently, the First Geneva Convention would likely not have been held either, attributing the creation of both to the aforementioned. With so much coming out of the works of men like Dunant, it is surprising that few books have been written about the influential philanthropist's life, though some do exist. Most of these books are short biographies such as the one written by Carol Zeman Rothkopf's, *Jean Henri Dunant: Father of the Red Cross*, published in 1969. Hers is a good accounting of his life with numerous details of his financial problems and eventual awarding of the Nobel Peace Prize in 1901 though little is added above the books and papers written about the creation of the organization itself.[10] Regardless of the amount of published works on Dunant, his importance in the creation of international humanitarian law cannot be dismissed. Much of the existing scholarship like Rothkopf's work on Dunant does a good job of exmplaining the man and his motivations, but there was little on his influences that helped bring him to the position of philanthropy that made him the man he was. This thesis will look deeper into the man to identify his driving force and exactly how the Battle of Solferino changed him from a businessman into a philanthropist above all else.

Like the men involved, not much has been written about the First Geneva Convention either. Minutes from the first meeting exist and the published document that was signed by those in attendance is on display, but little has been written about the meeting itself. The majority of interest in the Geneva Conventions stems from the meetings in 1949 following the Second World War. While there are numerous papers and books written about those conventions, only a few exist detailing the events of the first meeting. The most significant outcome from that first meeting was the creation of the committee that would become the International Committee of the Red Cross, which was written about in great detail in John Hutchinson's book, *Champions of Charity: War and the Rise of the Red Cross*. Hutchinson spares no detail in discussing the creation of the organization as well as Moynier and Dunant's parts in doing so. He describes Dunant's witnessing of the Battle of Solferino as a "Happy accident" that serendipitously initiated a cause for change on an international level.[11]

Francis Lieber's Lieber Code was an incredibly influential entry into the world of humanitarianism that is described well in John Catalano's, *Francis Lieber: Hermeneutics and Practical Reason*, which not only goes into an excellent biography of Lieber, but also goes into the nature of the code, how it came to be, how it was used. The work is predominantly philosophical and is informative as to the nature of the code. One of the best narratives of the code itself can be found in Gary D. Solis,' *The Law of Armed Conflict: International humanitarian Law in War*, where he goes into great detail about the Lieber Code and its influence on international humanitarian law.[12] These books and others are excellent accounts of both the importance of the Lieber Code and its impact on international humanitarian law, but there is little to no mention of the relationship between the impetus for the drafting of the Code and the need to justify freeing the slaves. Those connections will be made in this thesis.

There are thousands of excellent books that go into the history of the Civil War and this thesis will only briefly touch on the basics of the conflict as it pertained to both battlefield medicine and prisoners of war. One of the most comprehensive books about the Civil War is James McPherson's, *Battle Cry of Freedom: The Civil War Era*, which was published in 1988, but still holds true as one of the best histories of the war. The book goes into extraordinary detail about every aspect of the war including the causes for it, which many historians have debated for the past 150 years though almost all agree that the issue of slavery and its expansion were the primary instigator for the war, as well as several pages about the prisoner of war camps like Andersonville.[13] The literature covering the Civil War prisons is extensive and covers a wide range of topics. Historians that have written about the camps following the war have focused a great deal of attention on Andersonville with slightly less work being done on Camp Douglas and other Union prisoner of war camps. Though extensive in its coverage of the war, the most informative book on Andersonville is the novel of the same name by MacKinlay Kantor. *Andersonville* is actually a work of fiction, but was based on more than twenty-five years of research by the author who tells a heartbreaking story of the men inside the camp, those living just outside it, and the ongoing struggles between the two. Because it is a work of historical fiction, it is something that should be read to get a better understanding of the prison, but should be put aside for Robert Scott Davis', *Andersonville Civil War Prison*, a concise and detailed telling of the horrors of the camp. Scott makes a case for the nature of Wirz's position in the camp and his use as a scapegoat calling him "The right man in the wrong place."[14] This book helps to isolate the issue of accountability and blame following the revelation of atrocity to the North. The book covers in great detail the trial of Wirz and identifies the nature of the claims made against him. As the only officer tried, convicted, and executed of war crimes following the war, Henry Wirz remains a prominent figure in Civil War history. Scott does a good job in covering his work at the camp, capture, trial, and execution.

Like Andersonville, much has been written about Camp Douglas. One of the most interesting accounts of the camp are found in Kelly Pucci's, *Camp Douglas: Chicago's Civil War Prison*, which features pictures from the period with explanations of each. Pucci's book is good in showing an illustrated narrative of the people involved and life in the camp in Chicago, but lacks as much detail as David L. Keller's, *The Story of Camp Douglas: Chicago's Forgotten Civil War Prison*, a detailed historical accounting of Camp Douglas comparable to Davis' work on Andersonville. Keller conducts a detailed analysis of Camp Douglas and covers an interesting aspect; how the local Chicagoans felt about the camp and what was being done to the Confederate prisoners within.[15] Keller also analyzes the high death-rate of prisoners at Camp

Douglas and discusses what the principal causes were. His analysis is detailed and objective making it an excellent secondary source for a study of both Camp Douglas and Civil War prisons in general. It is important to understand the various atrocities committed at these camps so that the need for change is apparent in analyzing the aftermath of the camps and their effect on those who would eventually push for new laws and regulations to help protect soldiers captured as prisoners of war.

In their book, *Transforming Civil War Prisons: Lincoln, Lieber, and the Politics of Captivity*, Paul J. Springer and Glenn Robins examine the nature of civil war imprisonment and how the use of specific locations, politics, disease, and the experiences of the captive helped to shape the nature of the conflict. They also discuss how the treatment of prisoners of war during the American Civil War.[16]

Like the Civil War, there have been many published articles and books covering the Geneva Conventions of 1949. The minutes from the meetings, the published documents, and accounts from those present are easy to find and review. Some of the more detailed works that analyze the conventions and their impact on international humanitarian law are Solis' previously mentioned *The Law of Armed Conflict: International Humanitarian Law in War*, Eve La Haye's, *War Crimes in Internal Armed Conflicts*, Durham and McCormack's, *The Changing Face of Conflict and the Efficacy of International Humanitarian Law*, all of which offer extensive analyses of the conventions and their use in internal and external conflicts.

The works described in this literature review and those found in the bibliography are only a small sampling of the vast amount of data pertaining to the American Civil War, Geneva Conventions, Prisoner of War Camps, and the International Committee of the Red Cross. The Civil War is a perennial favorite of American historians, but the vast amount of detail neglects to connect the various atrocities of the conflict with America's involvement in the First (and subsequent) Geneva Conventions. While each work accounts for specific details to a particular person, organization, or event; little is done to properly connect those to American involvement so this study intends to ascertain the connection and nature of American involvement in the creation of international humanitarian law.

JEAN-HENRI DUNANT & THE BATTLE OF SOLFERINO

"Thus, a single individual, inspired with the sentiment of kindness and compassion for his fellow-creatures, by his own untiring energy attained the realization of his ideas, and aided in the progress of mankind toward peace."[17]

While little was done prior to the creation of the Red Cross to bring about serious change when it came to the care of captured and wounded soldiers, there were a few people who were aware of the problems on the battlefields of Europe and sought change. Of all the people who took part in the creation of the International Committee of the Red Cross and the Geneva Conventions that followed, none were as important as Jean-Henri Dunant. Dunant's work in humanitarian relief and international aid was so important, it is possible that nothing would exist today like the Geneva Conventions, Red Cross, and Red Crescent. His work was so important and instrumental in changing the world for the better that it is necessary to ascertain how he went from being a man more interested in his own affairs to the man who ended up caring for anyone in need of help that he could provide.

Born in Geneva, Switzerland in May of 1828, Dunant was educated in a devoutly Calvinist upbringing that stressed the importance on social work within his community.[18] His first three decades were spent in education and some minor philanthropic work, which included the establishment of several committees and organizations such as the first Geneva branch of the YMCA, which was initially a member of the Christian Union of Young People.[19] He eventually got into banking, a credible professions for a man of his upbringing in Geneva. Because of his work in the banking industry, he was often sent to work in North Africa to represent European business interests there. While on one of these trips, he wrote his first publication, "A travel book on Tunis that contained an interesting account of Muslim culture."[20] He also included a chapter on Muslim slavery in the region and would become a staunch abolitionist who would eventually work alongside Harriet Beecher Stowe.[21] Dunant would later form his own company after acquiring a profitable tract of land in French-occupied Algiers. He made a journey to Paris to meet with Napoleon III, a leader whom Denton admired greatly, to secure the water-usage rights necessary to farm the land. Finding that the Emperor and his army had set out for Italy, Denton followed after them making his way towards Solferino.[22] Dunant's life was forever altered when he visited the battlefield of Solferino on the 24th of June, 1859, just one day following a battle that left more than 40,000 men wounded and dying.[23]

The Battle of Solferino was the final engagement between the combined forces of the French and Sardinian armies against the Austrian Army. With some 300,000 participants, it was the largest battle of the Second Italian War of Independence and the last battle in history to be commanded by each army's personal monarchs.[24] The battle was somewhat of a surprise for the opposing forces. They had gathered and marched into one another accidentally after all efforts at reconnaissance the previous day had falsely revealed the location of each army. As the two forces approached one another, they came upon each other suddenly and in surprise, having been misinformed by their scouts that only a small part of the allied army had crossed the Chiese River.[25] Adversely, the Franco-Sardinian forces had also been falsely informed of their opponent's intentions and the two armies clashed with little preparation. Because the Austrian army was so fatigued as a result of their all-night march towards the enemy, they were ill-equipped to take the fight to the allies. Additionally, they had "to suffer from the intensely hot weather as well as from hunger and thirst."[26] With opposing lines of battle stretching ten miles with 300,000 men, the fighting was intense. Dunant provides a detailed account of the battle, though he was not present to witness it and only arrived at its conclusion. It was what he saw in the fields of battle that pushed him towards action. Having arrived in the aftermath, he noted that there were whole battalions without food and water. Dunant wrote about the silence of the night being broken as he "heard groans, stifled cries of anguish and pain, and heartrending voices calling for help."[27] His description of the various injuries and maladies of those injured is descriptive and detailed. Dunant describes the confusion of the battle and the lack of care provided to the injured having seen "inexpressible despair and suffering of every kind."[28]

Seeing thousands of men dying in the field without anyone attending them to provide aid or comfort, Dunant made for the closest city of Castiglione and encouraged the citizens to help him provide aid. He worked tirelessly for three days straight to assist the men of both sides of the conflict. His descriptive detail of the types of wounds and the implements that caused them are compelling. In addition to his mention of the battle and its aftermath, he also accounts for the care of the wounded that would follow. He describes a total of 40,000 killed and wounded and summarized the battle as a humanitarian crisis. Lacking a traditional military point-of-view, Dunant describes the Battle of Solferino as both a humanitarian and a European catastrophe."[29] This statement is significant in that it would help to fuel his ambition towards humanitarian aid that he would seek for the remainder of his life.

Figure 1. ICRC, *After the Battle of Solferino*. 1859, Digital, 520 x 353 pix. The International Committee of the Red Cross, Geneva, Switzerland. Available from: ICRC, https://www.icrc.org/ (accessed 11 June, 2015).

It was because of the horrors he witnessed that he felt compelled in 1862, while living in Geneva, to write about the battle. Inarguably his most significant work, *Un Souvenir de Solferino*, not only details an account of the battle and its aftermath, but it also established the need for a recognized humanitarian aid organization that would eventually be established as the International Committee of the Red Cross. His book furnishes a question that is used in both the formation of the ICRC as well as the Geneva Conventions that would follow.[30] Most notable, the question pertained to the possibility to establish an aid society that could "provide, during war, volunteer nurses for the wounded, without distinction of nationality?"[31] Such an organization had never truly existed previously and creating it would require a great deal of work and sacrifice by each and every nation involved in international conflict.

THE INTERNATIONAL COMMITTEE OF THE RED CROSS

"To protect the lives and dignity of victims of armed conflict and violence and to provide them with assistance."[32]

Before anything could be done to bring some element of peace and humanity to the suffering men on the battlefields of the world, it was necessary to create an internationally-recognized organization whose sole purpose was for the care of the sick, wounded, and dying. This organization needed to not only be something agreed-upon by any and all nations of the world, but it needed to be internationally recognized and granted both a status of neutrality and one of neutrality so that it could operate with impunity ensuring that the men and women who volunteered their services would not come under harm so close to the fighting that was happening throughout the world. The organization that was formed to answer this call was to be called the International Committee of the Red Cross and it would enter into service successfully and remain so to this day.

The International Committee of the Red Cross can trace its roots to the book published by Dunant accounting his actions following the Battle of Solferino. Having published the book himself and distributed it directly to people whom he felt could possible take action on his question mentioned at the end of the previous chapter, the book found its way to the desk of Gustave

Moynier, the president of the Geneva society for Public Utility (SGUP).[33] Moynier was so taken by the content of the book and the final passages asking for prominent people to create some sort of aid organization, he called upon Dunant to discuss his plans. Learning quickly from the meeting that Dunant was more of an idealist than an organizer, Moynier decided to bring up the idea of an internationally-recognized aid organization made up of volunteers at the next meeting of the SGUP, "In order to gauge by the reaction of its members—all of them men of affairs—whether such a proposal was feasible and worth pursuing further."[34]

On the 9th of February, 1863, Moynier raised the idea at a meeting of the SGUP and the majority of members agreed upon pursuing the matter further. A committee of five men to include Moynier, General Dufour, Dr. Appia, Dr. Maunoir, and Dunant was formed to determine the practicality of creating a volunteer organization along the lines proposed by Dunant in his book.[35] General Guillaume Henri Dufour was the hero of the Sonderbund War of 1847 and had a great deal of influence on Emperor Napoleon III, whom he once tutored.[36] Doctor Théodore Maunoir was a distinguished surgeon who had been president of the Geneva Medical Society twice was both a great philanthropist and knowledgeable of the various conflicts of the English-speaking world such as the American Civil War. Doctor Louis Appia was the sitting president of that same society and was also the protégé of Dr. Maunoir.[37]

The first meeting was a fruitful one that ultimately separated the five into a permanent committee independent of the AGUP. The primary goal of this newly-formed committee would be to "encourage each nation, each region, and even each city to create whatever sort of committee seemed appropriate in the circumstances."[38] Subsequent meetings were conducted that eventually addressed the need for an international conference to bring together influential people from throughout Europe. Moynier and Dunant had already created a draft of ten articles addressing the various needs the men had discussed over the months. These ten articles would eventually be finalized at the idealized meeting, which would eventually be called the First Geneva Convention. While the various European participants found their way to Geneva via membership in the AGUP and through invitation of their members, the delegates from the United States of America would arrive as outsiders to the main group. Having no participation in the various conflicts of Europe that had been ongoing for some time, the Americans were concerned with their own struggle that had been running since 1861, the American Civil War.

The American Civil War was nearing its bloodiest days when the first meeting took place that would create the International Committee of the Red Cross. Within a few months, the two great armies of the United States and confederacy would clash in Gettysburg, Pennsylvania, and it would become all too apparent that a need existed to bring some level of relief to the great suffering that accompanied that and many other horrible battles. It would not be until long after the war's conclusion that the United States would be able to establish an American Red Cross, but the need was apparent for change and President Lincoln began to make strides to incorporate both a new law of war and a listing of rules that would help bring some element of humanitarianism to the ongoing conflict.[39] Lincoln would eventually call for a new code of rules to address these issues and would further his plans for emancipation of the slaves as well, all of which were intricately tied together in an unforgiving landscape of politics, fear, and warfare.

THE LIEBER CODE & THE PROBLEM OF EMANCIPATION

"This code has remained the basis of all subsequent efforts in the direction of the humanization of war."[40]

      The United States made an innovation in the creation of a new codex of laws regulating the behavior of the military in enemy territory. The Lieber Code would become the United States' first major attempt at an international treaty concerning the conduct of its military and it helped to bridge the gap that brought the United States to the Geneva Convention. The Code was the first attempt by any nation to establish the laws of war in a way that the men involved might be held accountable and it greatly influenced the people in Geneva who were paying attention to international military affairs such as Denton. Originally titled *Instructions for the Government of Armies of the United States in the Field; General Order no. 100*, the code was promulgated by President Abraham Lincoln as well as his officers. While it only applied to members of the United States military, it was used heavily throughout the remaining two years of the war as not only a guide for future battles, but also as a means to hold people accountable for their actions should they violate the code.

      The most interesting aspect of the Lieber Code has to do with when and why it was commissioned by President Lincoln. Only 10 of the 157 articles in the Code have to deal with the issue of emancipation, but these 10 articles are the only ones that are truly revolutionary, unique, and controversial. Ever since the War of 1812, it had been common practice in Western warfare to refrain from freeing captured slaves so that they could fight against their former masters. This practice stemmed from thousands of years of history wherein servile wars of insurrection were often the bloodiest and most horrific conflicts to embattle a civilized nation.[41] Because of the fear of a servile insurrection, it was considered uncivilized and often barbaric to allow former slaves to take up arms against those who enslaved them. The practice was ongoing for nearly a century in the Americas when Abraham Lincoln first thought to emancipate the slaves. There was even opposition amongst allies in the Union against freeing the slaves in an indiscriminate manner for "fear of servile insurrection, which conjured images of mutilation, pillage, torture, and rape."[42]

The issue of emancipation during the American Civil War was first raised in a real manner by John Charles Frémont, a Union Army commander of the Armies of the West who gained notoriety when he emancipated the slaves in his territory without first consulting with the President or any other members in his chain of command. He was reprimanded and relieved for this, mostly due to the concern the South would have about the potential for a servile insurrection. Lincoln recognized the need to conduct the business of emancipation in a manner that was legal, safe, and beneficial to the war effort. As a result, he commissioned Francis Lieber to draft his famous code.

The Lieber Code was authored by Francis Lieber, a political philosopher and German immigrant who opposed secession and spoke against it while living in South Carolina before the outbreak of the war.[43] He eventually joined the war effort on the side of the north and worked for the War Department under President Lincoln. Lieber was considered by many to be a revolutionary who balked at the tradition of moral structure in warfare in favor of military necessity. Lieber argued that anything should be allowed in warfare so long as it benefited the necessity of the military forces conducting the campaign. This was indeed revolutionary in the nineteenth century and is today considered to be relatively barbaric. Article 15 specifically addressed the term 'military necessity' by allowing for the willful and direct destruction of the life (or limb) of a nation's enemies with allowances for those whose destruction is considered to be unavoidable in the act of combat. This essentially allowed for a military to conduct itself without fear of reprisal from the death of noncombatants who may have been caught in the middle of a conflict. This practice differs significantly from how warfare has since evolved to limit, as much as possible, the instance of collateral damage. The article further describes the ability and allowance for a military to capture armed personnel, destroy their property, means of travel and communication, as well as the deliberate withholding of subsistence to the enemy, whether captured or still engaged.[44] This article in particular can be considered immoral in application, yet it allows for the ease of operation of a military force in any situation and is considered to be a fundamental, if not unforgivable, law of war.

In continuance of Lieber's justifications of emancipation due to military necessity, he explains succinctly the nature of slavery and property by saying in Article 42 that slavery is recognized only in local municipal law and that the laws of nations and nature do not acknowledge it. Furthermore, he cites Roman law that explains all men are equal and uses these justifications to explain that fugitives who have escaped from a nation in which they were considered criminals, serfs, or slaves would be freed and acknowledged as free citizens regardless of the enslavement laws of their former nation. In the following article he then explains that any former slave who had escaped from bondage in the Confederacy to the separate country of the United States would therefore be "Entitled to the rights and privileges of a freeman" and continues to state that returning that person to a state of slavery would "amount to enslaving a free person, and neither the United States nor any officer under their authority can enslave and human being."[45] Through these two articles, Lieber is able to not only justify the legality of emancipation, but also terminate the rights of property of former slave owners over the newly-freed slaves. This is incredibly significant because it directly addressed the concerns of emancipation and the supposed 'barbarism' of the abolishment of the historical practice of maintaining a captured slave's status to avoid a servile insurrection. Regardless of the remaining articles of the Lieber Code, President Lincoln specifically required these justifications so that he could push the country towards the path of emancipation. The Lieber Code was first published on the 24th of April, 1862, but it was written and circulated amongst the top officials of the Union since December of the previous year. By releasing it in April, Lincoln was able to use it as a means of justifying and enforcing his famous Emancipation Proclamation.[46]

President Lincoln published the Emancipation Proclamation on the 1st of January, 1863. While the document did not end slavery in the United States, it did terminate it in the states that seceded from the Union and formed the Confederacy. This carried no weight during the war since the Confederacy didn't recognize its legality on their sovereign states, but it did allow for the liberation of slaves in the states that had been captured by the Union. In January of 1863, this comprised of lands within much of Tennessee, Arkansas, Louisiana, Mississippi, and full control of the Mississippi River. The Proclamation was published with the goal of appeasing the abolitionists in the north as well as to curry favor with France and Great Britain who were potentially on the cusp of recognizing the Confederacy for their cotton exports. Lincoln hoped that slaves would rise up and fight against their masters once the Proclamation was signed, but the reality was that the slaves would only rise up once they were liberated by the North. When this happened, they flooded into the ranks of the military as well as into military support roles totaling some 200,000 by the end of the war. Lincoln knew that slavery was coming to an end and he knew that it was not something that could be undertaken in one broad measure. He was very careful about how this was handled and it was due to a series of steps that helped to bring about an end to slavery in the United States. Both the Lieber Code and the Emancipation Proclamation worked in tandem to make this a possibility and it helped lead to a Union victory.

One of the most problematic actions that the Lieber Code initiated was the cessation of prisoner transfers and trades between the two nations. Prior to the enactment of the Code, the United States and Confederate States would engage in a transfer of prisoners of war in the manner accustomed to the times. When the Lieber Code was published with Article 49, everything changed. Article 49 is important because it identifies any armed combatant associated with a nation or military force to be equal under the law. "All soldiers of whatever species of arms; all men who belong to the rising en masse of the hostile country....all disabled men or officers on the field or elsewhere, if captured....have thrown away their arms and ask for quarter, are prisoners of war....entitled to the privileges of a prisoner of war."[47] This article essentially demands that whether a soldier is black or white, they were to be considered lawful combatants who were engaged in their nations' business of war and should be treated as such. The problem was that the South refused to consider black soldiers fighting against them on the side of the Union as soldiers and instead considered them to be nothing more than criminals, akin to escaped slaves deserving only to be either executed on the spot or returned to a state of enslavement.

President Jefferson Davis issued General Orders, No. 111 on the 24th of December, 1862; a now infamous proclamation that arose following the occupation of the city of New Orleans by General Benjamin F. Butler, whom the Confederacy had come to call "The Beast." When General Butler first took command of the occupation of New Orleans, he established martial law and curtailed the citizens' freedoms of speech and movement. Life in the city became progressively harder for the people held within and Butler even turned on the local women by proclaiming that all women who insult or show contempt to any officer or soldier of the Union Army shall be treated as a woman "plying her avocation," meaning, they would be treated as a prostitute.[48] This order later became known as the 'woman order' for its targeting of women in New Orleans. The following illustration describes the nature and reception of Butler's order:

The Ladies of New Orleans before General Butler's Proclamation.   After General Butler's Proclamation.

Figure 2. John McLenan, *Harper's Weekly Political Cartoon*. July 12th, 1862, Digital, 1200 x 660 pix. The New York Times Company, New York, New York. Available from: NYTimes, https://www.nytimes.com/ (accessed 20 May, 2015).

The panel on the left shows the women of New Orleans spitting in the faces of the occupying Union soldiers while the one on the right shows them in a more pleasing manner, welcomed by the enemy soldier, behaving as a prostitute. Butler's actions were made due to the manner in which the white women of New Orleans treated his soldiers, many of whom were black. Because of this proclamation by Butler, he earned the ire of almost every member of the Confederacy to include President Davis. Davis recognized a need to address both the harsh treatment imposed by General Butler as well as the use of black soldiers by the Union Army. In response, he drafted his own General Order.

Like Butler's General Order, Davis' became infamous having several consequences both seen an unforeseen. Davis' General Order 111 accomplished two things: it addressed General Butler and his actions directly, and it established the future treatment of black Union Army soldiers captured in battle. Beginning the General Order, President Davis describes Butler and his subordinate officers as "an outlaw and common enemy of mankind" whom he further says should be hanged immediately upon capture. He furthers this by saying the same treatment shall be afforded to Butler's officers should they be captured. This basically established both Butler and his men as criminals and not recognized combatants who should be given quarter as prisoners of war. Davis then specifically addresses the perceived crimes done to the people of New Orleans. "The entire population of the city of New Orleans have been forced to elect between starvation....and taking an oath against conscience to bear allegiance to the invaders of their country."[49] He further describes the harsh treatment of women specifically and the nature of the slaves who were captured with the city. Butler initially considered the slaves to be 'confiscated property' and as such, kept the local economy in disarray. The most infamous passage from Davis' General Order established "That all Negro slaves captured in arms be at once delivered over to the executive authorities of the respective States to which they belong to be dealt with according to the laws of said States."[50] While this passage does not directly state that captured black soldiers would be executed, that was the practice that came from its drafting. The Union perceived it as such and the actions of the Confederacy thereafter supported this practice.

The clearest example of this occurred on the 12th of April, 1864 at Fort Pillow, Tennessee.

The Fort Pillow Massacre was a notorious event during the Civil War where approximately 600 Union soldiers were captured by the forces commanded under Confederate Major General Nathan B. Forrest. Nearly half of those captured were black soldiers who were summarily executed upon surrender. The incident was controversial and has been hotly debated by historians since the conclusion of the war. Most historians like Albert Castel and Andrew Ward have concluded that the black soldiers (as well as the white men) had surrendered and were no longer resisting when they were massacred by Forrest's troops. In some cases, the survivors stated that the Confederate troops were screaming "No quarter!" as they stabbed the black soldiers with their bayonets.[51]

THE FORT PILLOW MASSACRE.

Figure 3. Kurz & Allison, *The Fort Pillow Massacre*. 1892, Digital, 900 x 651 pix. The New fineArtAmerica, Santa Monica, California. Available from: fineArtAmerica, http://images.fineartamerica.com(accessed 13 June, 2015).

This event can be tied back to President Davis' General Order in a number of ways. Though it was originally ambiguous, the order essentially states that any black soldiers who were originally slaves should be dealt with in a manner befitting a runaway slave (criminal in the eyes of the Confederacy). Furthermore, the General Order does not make any distinction between freed men or those who were never enslaved in the first place and as a result, the Southern commanders could get away with treating these men in the same manner as they treated the slaves. It became a common practice to simply kill any black men wearing the uniform of the United States Army, which may have been the intent of Davis' General Order in the first place, but the actual consequence was relatively unforeseen for Davis.

President Davis likely thought that the threat of execution upon capture would keep large numbers of black men from enlisting into the Union Army, but the opposite was the case.[52] Regardless of what might happen once captured, there appeared to be a surge in black enlistments upon the publishing of Davis' General Order. Though it may have intended to prevent the rise of a servile insurrection and keep emancipation at bay, the General Order published by President Jefferson Davis actually helped to increase the chances for emancipation, or at the very least, push it closer to reality. The increase in black soldiers fighting for the Union and the publishing of both the Lieber Code and Davis' General Order No. 111 were instrumental in creating the problem that would bring the Civil War's treatment of prisoners of war into a humanitarian crisis. The main complication arose when the Confederacy refused to treat black soldiers as anything but criminals and would no longer trade them as equal for white soldiers in prisoner of war transfers. Because of this, the United States halted all prisoner of war transfers, which created its own unintended consequences.

With no means of reducing the populations of prisoners in the camps, both the north and the south were faced with the real problem of housing, feeding, and caring for their captured enemies. Throughout warfare, captured prisoners were afforded some humanitarian aid so that they could eventually be traded with the enemy for one's own men. When the prisoner transfers came to a halt, this created a situation wherein both side no longer needed to provide the necessary care to their captured soldiers such as had been done in previous conflicts. As a result, the camps at Andersonville and Chicago, New York, and elsewhere became impossible to manage and the reality of housing thousands of men in a small space for extended periods of time became a crisis that neither side knew how to manage.

PAROLE, FURLOUGHS, AND EXCHANGES

"The United States will throw its protection around all its officers and men without regard to color and will promptly retaliate for all cases violating the cartel or the laws and usages of war."[53]

The practice of paroling captured soldiers was utilized by both sides prior to the Lieber Code as a means of dealing with large numbers of personnel they were unable to handle. A parole would occur when captured soldiers were given notes of parole indicating they would no longer take part in the fight until they could be formally exchanged for captured soldiers. The newly-paroled soldiers would then return to their homes on furlough and would await a formal transfer.[54] This actually occurred prior to the beginning of the war when, on the 18th of February, 1861, Texas seceded and all of the Union forces in the State were surrendered to the Confederacy. Every soldier was granted a pardon and sent back to the north.[55]

This established a non-official precedent that was carried into the conflict beginning in Missouri where Confederate Brigadier General Gideon Johnson Pillow arranged for an informal exchange of prisoners with his opposing commander, Colonel William Hervey Lamme Wallace. The two sides bickered over the specifics of who could be transferred and the terms until finally, only six men were exchanged between the two forces.[56] This type of limited exchange would continue across the various battlefields between commanders without specific guidance from either Richmond or Washington, D.C.

One of the main reasons that the Lincoln Administration didn't publish specific orders regarding the exchange of prisoners was due to their refusal to recognize the Confederacy as being any type of legitimate government.[57] This policy would remain through to the end of 1861 as public opinion became louder and louder in opposition to the lack of a formal position concerning prisoner exchanges from the administration. Lincoln eventually acquiesced by first sending clothing and food through the front lines, though this operation was eventually recalled due to the desire for the Confederate emissaries' to negotiate an exchange policy with the two men sent with the provisions. It wasn't until the 23rd of June, 1862, that the Senate drafted a resolution to call for legitimizing a prisoner exchange. Lincoln then authorized Major General John Adams Dix to negotiate with Major General Daniel Harvey Hill to decide on a formal practice of prisoner exchange. The two men achieved an agreement, which would come to be called the Dix-Hill Cartel on the 22nd of July, 1863.[58]

The agreement between the two General officers allowed for a sliding-scale of worth given to enlisted men and officers with excess prisoners being authorized parole with the stipulation that they not be allowed to rejoin the fight until they could be properly and officially exchanged. Additionally, the agreement called for agents from each side to be appointed so that the process could be overseen in a friendly and bureaucratic manner. The Confederate agent was Robert Ould while the Union appointed Brigadier General Lorenzo Thomas.[59] The initial result was that both sides began to empty their prisons so that prisoners could be paroled and returned to their respective side. In many cases, the prisoners were aided and provided transportation by their former captors in a civilized manner suggesting each side knew the dangers of mistreating their captives for fear of the same happening to their comrades. By the 22nd of August, most of the northern prisons were emptied of their prisoners as groups as large as one thousand men each would march towards their homes.

This new system was beneficial to both sides, but also detrimental in a number of respects. The soldiers realized fairly quickly that they would no longer have to languish in an enemy prisoner of war camp for months on end and would instead be granted a parole, which gave them an extensive furlough until they were formally exchanged. In effect, this allowed for a soldier to be taken prisoner, granted a pardon, and given a furlough and a pass to go home for an extended period of time, removing them from the fight and returning them to their families. The first time this type of abuse was identified happened at the Battle of Shiloh where almost two thousand Union soldiers were taken prisoner and granted paroles in the field. This effectively took the men out of the fight, which created problems for the war department.

To combat this problem, the War Department issued a General Order, which called an end to furloughs for paroled prisoners. Instead of being allowed to return home until they could be properly exchanged, paroled prisoners were required to report to one of several facilities where they would wait until an exchange was made. One such camp, called Camp Chase in Columbia, Ohio took in men from Indiana, Kentucky, Michigan, Ohio, Tennessee, and Virginia while soldiers from Illinois, Iowa, Minnesota, Missouri, and Wisconsin were send to Benton Barracks outside of Saint Louis, Missouri. Soldiers from the east were sent to the aptly named Camp Parole outside of Annapolis, Maryland.[60] Most paroled soldiers went to the camps though some decided to evade desertion charges and avoided them. Because they were not authorized to perform any military duties, the parolees refused to perform their normal duties such as guard duty and the commandants of the camps reported numerous problems. Ultimately, it was determined that the parolee camps were no better than the camps the men would have been kept by the Confederacy and the camps began to refuse new parolees by September of 1862. In an ironic twist, the terms that allowed for an exchange of prisoners essentially meant that each side was now required to imprison their own personnel. The camps were poorly manned and maintained with little supplies entering on a regular basis. The parolees began to loot and pillage the surrounding towns and many of them devolved into criminal behavior. The problems in the north were mirrored in the south with thousands of men having been interred in poor conditions.

The Confederacy came to distrust the Union when it came to prisoner transfers and exchanges. In a letter to President Jefferson Davis, Colonel Robert Ould wrote that he believed the Federal Government did "not intend to keep faith with us in the matter of prisoners or exchanges."[61] Furthermore, he stressed that the Federals were using deceit and fraud to pull more exchanges out of the south than was equitable. He cited an example of 40 officers who had been held at Camp Chase beyond their agreed-upon release even though the government insisted this wasn't true. He also wrote of the Federal Government's written intention that it "was not the intention....to make any more arrests of noncombatants" in their territory though he stipulated that this practice had continued long beyond the letter's drafting.[62] Ould would continue to stress the failures of the Dix-Hill Cartel until it finally was abandoned by both sides.

The exchange finally came to an end when the Confederate Congress issued a joint resolution on the 1st of May, 1863, which declared that black soldiers who were captured in combat would be turned over to the states to be returned to slavery.[63] This was the final straw in the cartel and it led to its demise. Because the United States would not accept that black soldiers were unequal to whites, they argued that "the United States will throw its protection around all its officers and men without regard to color and will promptly retaliate for all cases violating the cartel or the laws and usages of war."[64] This stipulation effectively halted all prisoner exchanges throughout the United States and Confederate States of America, which led to the problem of the then empty prisoner of war camps returning to a state of overpopulation, malnutrition, and disease.

UNION ARMY PRISONER OF WAR CAMPS

"I wondered what caused all of this fearful mortality. . . . Was it starvation, neglect, and cruelty? God alone knows."[65]

Following the closure of the camps when the prisoner transfers began, they were repurposed to house the returned soldiers who were no longer allowed a furlough. After this period passed with the Confederacy's rejection of black Union soldiers being allowed transfer, the camps were again repurposed back into standard prisoner of war camps, though the conditions were rarely made better and were in fact, made worse by many measures. When the camps were meant for paroled soldiers, they were left somewhat open with the men being allowed to patronize the local shops and bars, but closing the camps for actual prisoners of war meant that this was no longer an option. Often, this resulted in less food and supplies for the incarcerated soldiers as well as serious problems of overcrowding. Most camps were built for other purposes and were not equipped to house the influx of personnel that were coming to them in 1863 so the problems leading to a humanitarian crisis within began to escalate.

The Union had dozens of camps, some of which were temporary while others were permanent locales that were established either for the purpose of housing prisoners of war or were meant for other military means. The largest and most distressed camps were Camp Chase outside of Columbus, Ohio (E), Camp

Douglas outside of Chicago, Illinois (A), Elmira Prison outside of Elmira, New York (C), Fort Deleware on Pea Patch Island, Deleware (D), and Point Lookout in Maryland (B).[66]

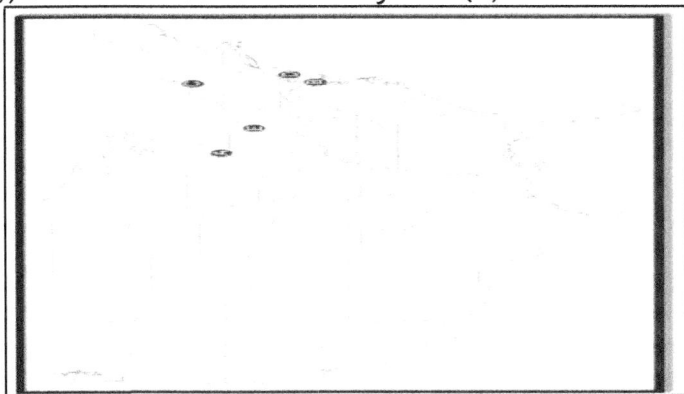

Figure 4. National Cemetery Administration, *Five largest Northern Prisoner of War (POW) Camps during the Civil War by mortality rates.* n.d., Digital, 458 × 247 pix. The National Park Service, Washington, D.C. Available from: NPS.gov, http://www.nps.gov/ (accessed 28 May, 2015).

Camp Chase was established in 1861 as a military staging and training camp with a small section planned for the incarceration of Confederate prisoners of war. Like the other camps throughout the north, Camp Chase had several problems that couldn't be solved easily; the worst of which was mud. Camp Chase was so encompassed with mud, it became the major complaint from Union and Confederates alike. One soldier, Jonathan Harrington, described the camps as being "nothing but a regular mortar bed, the mud is from four to six inches deep."[67] The mud was caused by the constant wet weather problematic in the region with repeated freezing and thawing cycles. As time progressed in the prison, the situation became worse and eventually, untenable. By February, 1863, Lieutenant J. K. Ferguson said that it had become so muddy that it was nearly impossible to move about the prison.[68] The mud caused a great deal of problems, the most of which concerned the health of the men who were staying there.

Disease was running rampant through the camp and the Union Army officials in charge of sanitation called the prisoner of war camp incapable of supporting anyone. Continued lack of funding and an influx of prisoners only exacerbated the problem. Among the diseases prevalent in Camp Chase, Typhoid, Smallpox, Dysentery, and Malaria were some of the worst. By the end of the war, more than 2,200 men died in Camp Chase. The camp was never meant to house more than 1,200 men but peaked at over 9,400. With such poor conditions throughout the camp and little to no money coming in from the Union to support the men incarcerated there, Camp Chase devolved from a military encampment with a small prisoner of war stockade into a full-blown concentration camp where men were taken off of the battlefield and sent to languish and die in the supposed care of the Union army. In many ways, Camp Chase was a terrible place to be sent, but many more suffered when they arrived at Camp Douglas.

Camp Douglas was also established early in the war to act as a supply and training location with a stockade built for incarcerated Union soldiers. The stockade eventually became a location for more than just arrested Union soldiers when the parole system was put into place and the formerly-furloughed soldiers were required to remain there. Following the breakup of the parole system, the camp was largely converted to a prisoner of war camp and quickly became one of the worst ones in the war.

When the conflict began, Camp Douglas was established and run with little problem due to the Union forces staying there having an ample supply of water and space for their training and housing needs. This continued until the Union defeated the Confederacy at the Battle of Fort Donelson and Fort Henry, which brought an influx of nearly 15,000 Confederate soldiers that required housing. The Camp outside of Chicago was able to take approximately 4,500 prisoners who were then housed at the small camp alongside their Union adversaries. At first, the two groups coexisted with people coming from the surrounding area to look into the camp and gaze at the captured soldiers. This didn't last for very long because the camp was only capable of housing approximately 9,000 people without first accounting for the needed personnel required for maintaining a prison. As the numbers increased and more and more captured Rebels were brought to Camp Douglas, the situation worsened and the camp went from being primarily used for the training of new recruits to a prisoner of war camp more akin to a concentration camp.

Figure 5. Camp Douglas Restoration Foundation, *Men enlisted at Camp Douglas, c. 1864*. Jun 29, 2012, Digital, 653 × 367 pix. National Broadcast Corporation Chicago, Chicago, Illinois. Available from: NBCChicago.com, http://media.nbcchicago.com (accessed 1 June, 2015).

As the above picture indicates, overcrowding quickly became a serious problem throughout the camp. The picture was taken in 1864, which was not even the height of camp occupation.

Unfortunately for the United States, their continued victories along the Mississippi River brought the problem of Confederate prisoners into the north with no means to house or clothe them. The winter of 1861-1862 was particularly harsh, especially in the Chicago area and this did not help the prison population at Camp Douglas. The conditions at the camp were continuing to worsen during the cartel period where the prisoners of war were less members of the Confederacy and more so member of the Union on parole. The camp's numbers continued to increase and after the parole system broke down and the Union soldiers were freed, the camp opened up to a massive influx of captured Rebels. By February of 1862, the camp was largely abandoned by the Union with only around 500 remaining to man the prison. The majority of the prison population was reduced to enlisted men with the officers having been transferred to Camp Chase.[69]

The United States Sanitary Commission, which would eventually attend the First Geneva Convention in Switzerland the following year, send the commission president, Henry W. Bellows, to Camp Douglas on the 30th of June, 1862 to make a detailed report of the conditions of the camp. He found the camp to be in a deplorable state. In a letter to Colonel Hoffman, the Acting Assistant Adjutant-General and camp commander, he wrote that "the place is as desperately circumstanced as any camp ever was.... The amount of standing water, of unpoliced grounds, of foul sinks, of unventilated and crowded barracks, of general disorder, of soil reeking with miasmatic accretions, of rotten bones and the emptyings of camp-kettles is enough to drive a sanitarian to despair."[70] He also described the incredible amount of vermin and excrement without any place to dispose of it further. He noted that ventilation and drainage were such a problem that a pestilence would surely grip the camp within the month.[71] Bellows' report was both detested and feared by the camp commander such that he dared Bellows to release it after he was accused by the Sanitation Committee president of a cover-up.[72] Because of this contention, Bellows did not release the report due to his presiding over a private organization that required the support of the administration. Without the support from Washington, the Sanitation Commission would no longer carry any weight. He proposed the planning and building of a hospital and new barracks, but Colonel Hoffman never embraced the plans, mostly due to a lack of funds. 1862 ended with a total of 980 deaths in the camp, 2 of which were killed by guards in confrontations, 1 was killed by another inmate, and 977 perished due to disease.[73] The diseases most prevalent were Typhoid Fever, Diphtheria, Smallpox, Cholera, Consumption (Tuberculosis), Dysentery, Measles, and Pneumonia; all of which are generally preventable given adequate food, water, and housing from the elements, but when those basic needs aren't met, these highly-contagious diseases spread rampant throughout the camp.[74]

The lack of funding for the camp was a serious problem that left many of the captured soldiers without anything to wear. Due in large part to the freezing temperatures and inadequate housing, hundreds died from exposure to the elements alone. "The mercury often fell to 20 degrees below zero" according to one Confederate soldier who was kept at the camp.[75] In February of 1863, the official count of the dead was at 387 as a result of the cold.[76] Most men had little to no clothing having been brought to the camp with whatever they had on them when they were captured. Most didn't have any sort of uniform and the clothing they did have was never washed, torn, rotten, and in many cases tattered beyond use. Reporters from the Chicago Sun Times reported that they observed men wearing sack cloths, potato bags, and many were even shirtless. After the winter months, the problem of the elements somewhat subsided, though due to the thaw cycle and poor sanitary conditions of the camp, the prisoners saw an increase in otherwise preventable diseases such as Typhus and Dysentery. Medical treatment at the camp was severely lacking with little room for hospital beds and inadequate medical personnel on hand.

Medical care at the camp was mostly absent though several aid organizations in and around Chicago came to the camp to provide care when and where they could. Thousands of dollars in donations were provided to the camp via these organizations, but little was effectively done due to the overcrowding. With diseases running rampant, one of the worst problems was starvation and scurvy, which was associated with the lack of food due to little Vitamin C in the inmates' diets. With conditions as they were, some prisoners attempted to escape whenever possible. At one point in November of 1863, seventy-five men were able to tunnel under the walls and escape. This made matters worse as the military response was to send eight companies of the Veteran Reserve Corps as well as a small contingent of sharpshooters from Michigan to better protect the camp's perimeter. With more Union forces in the area, the problem of starvation only increased as the Union soldiers were fed before the prisoners saw rations of any kind. Following this successful escape, no further tunnels were dug and more men continued to perish in the harsh and unruly conditions at Camp Douglas.

In addition to the problem of supplies, the ability to feed the prisoners as well as the guards became a consistent problem. As the camp underwent personnel changes with a half-dozen different commanders taking the helm between 1861 and 1865, the reasons for most of the problems were due to a lack of leadership, supplies, and ability to care for the men. The United States War Department continually assessed Camp Douglas at various states of ineptitude and attempted to fix the problem through the United States Sanitation Committee as well as via its own devices, but the camp would never fully support the men it came to house. By the end of the Civil War, Camp Douglas had claimed the lives of more than six thousand Confederate soldiers. The site has the following monument, which reads, 'To the Memory of the Six Thousand Southern Soldiers Here Buried Who Died in Camp Douglas Prison 1862-1865:'

Figure 6. C. B. Pritchett, *Camp Douglas Memorial in Chicago*. n.d., Digital, 560 × 260 pix. C. B. Pritchett, Washington, D.C. Available from: NCGenWeb.com, http://www.ncgenweb.us/transylvania/images/CampDouglasMemorial.jpg (accessed 1 June, 2015).

The horrific conditions at Camp Douglas as well as other Union installations like Camp Chase, Elmira Prison, Fort Delaware, and Point Lookout weighed heavily on the minds of the men who would eventually go to Geneva to join in the international conference that would become the First Geneva Convention as well as the International Committee of the Red Cross. After having witnessed the horrors of the camp, Henry W. Bellows' report on the conditions and atrocities noted there were not made public, but were available to men like Charles S. P. Bowles who would attend the First Geneva Convention on behalf of the United States of America in 1864. The work of the United States Sanitation Commission may not have aided the imprisoned Confederates at Camp Douglas in time to save any of the men, but it would go on to aid in the overall international concern of what was to become a humanitarian crisis of the American Civil War and bring the United States into international humanitarian relief organizations and efforts.

CONFEDERATE ARMY PRISONER OF WAR CAMPS

"Can see the dead wagon loaded up with twenty or thirty bodies at a time, two lengths, just like four foot wood is loaded on to a wagon at the North, and away they go to the grave yard on a trot. Perhaps one or two will fall off and get run over. No attention paid to that; they are picked up on the road back after more. Was ever before in this world anything so terrible happening? Many entirely naked."[77]

As bad as the situation in the north became, it quickly deteriorated in the south and was, by many accounts much worse. While the Confederates imprisoned in the north had to deal with the dangers of the damp and freezing climate, the United States soldiers in the south were attacked by the heat, humidity, and mosquitos they were unfamiliar with in their northern homeland. Just as the cold can bring on deadly consequences, so can continued exposure to moist, warm climates and this was certainly the case for thousands of Union Army officers and enlisted men imprisoned throughout the Confederacy.

The Confederacy had to deal with the outcome of the Lieber code and the North's refusal to continue prisoner transfers following the Confederate decision to refuse equal treatment for black prisoners of war by housing a large influx of Union soldiers. Just as the north had to compensate for the large numbers of Confederate prisoners, the southerners were likewise saddled with numbers they couldn't accommodate. Even with a large number of prisons spread throughout their territory, the Confederacy still failed to maintain the prisoners they were able to capture. Some of the largest prisons were Andersonville outside of Andersonville, Georgia, Belle Isle outside of Richmond, Virginia, Cahaba Prison near Selma, Alabama, Camp Ford near Tyler, Texas, and Libby Prison near Richmond, which was only for officers.

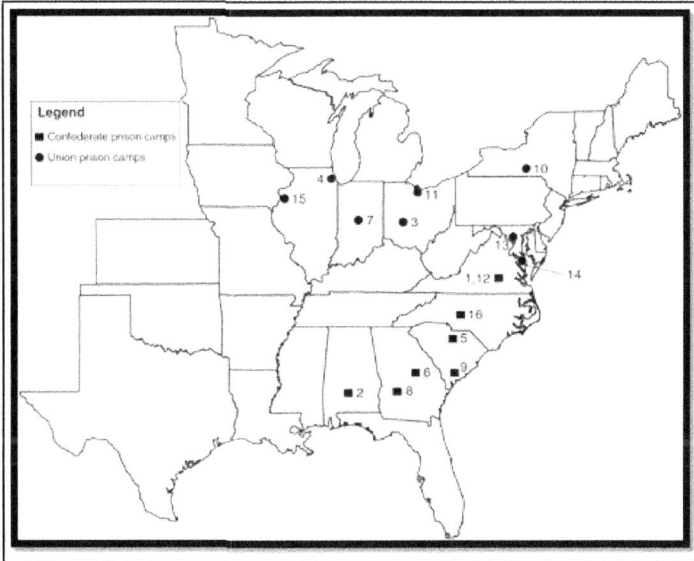

Figure 7. Richard Jensen, *Map of All Camps*. n.d., Digital, 463 × 351 pix. University of Illinois, Chicago, Illinois, Available from: Tigger.UIC.edu, http://tigger.uic.edu/ (accessed 1 June, 2015).

The above picture depicts the largest camps for each side. Andersonville is located at position number eight indicated by a square in southern Georgia.

While the Confederacy had no shortage of prisoner of war camps, few regard as much mention as Andersonville, the current site of the National Prisoner of War Museum and a registered National Historic Site. Andersonville was established and opened in February of 1864 so that a suitable location could be made further south than Virginia where it would be easier to house, feed, and care for the captured Union soldiers. The site that was chosen outside of Andersonville, Georgia comprised some 16.5 acres of land, which wasn't entirely flat and sloped to the south.

There was a stream that ran through the entire area and it was believed that it would provide sufficient water for consumption as well as for bathing to the men brought there. To make room for the prisoners, all of the trees within the stockade were felled and were used to create the stockade wall, which was uniformly 15 feet high and shaped in a rectangle about the camp. With all of the trees removed, there was no natural shade within the enclosure to act as any type of shelter. This was a serious problem for the men who would arrive en-masse in February, 1864 before the camp was fully equipped. Within three months, there were approximately 12,000 Union soldiers held at the camp. With no shelter to house them, they erected makeshift hovels with the detritus and debris of the stockade using anything they had to protect themselves from the harsh heat. Moldy and tattered blankets would enshroud crude shelters, which only became rotten when the rain came, which was often. When there was no debris left to build anything out of, the soldiers dug holes for them to get a modicum of shelter from the elements. The following depicts the dangers of such a lack of shelter:

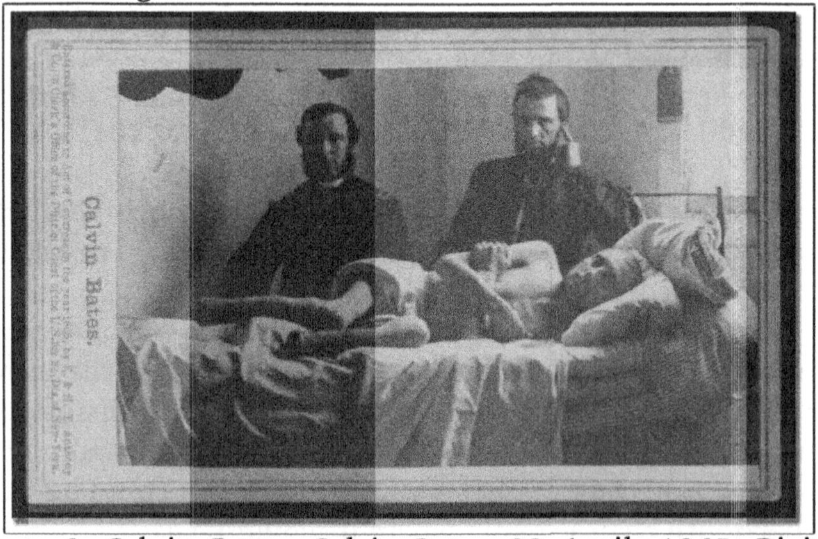

Figure 8. Calvin Bates, *Calvin Bates*. 28 April, 1865, Digital, 1,024 × 635 pix. Library of Congress, Washington D.C., Available from: CivilWarTalk.com, http://civilwartalk.com (accessed 2 June, 2015).

The preceding image is of Corporal Calvin Bates of Company E, 20th Regiment, Main, Volunteers who was captured at the Battle of Wilderness in May, 1864. He was imprisoned in Andersonville from the 23rd of May until the 12th of September, 1864 and swore on official records that "he and his fellow prisoners were totally unprovided with any shelter from the inclemency of the weather" save for what they brought or were able to produce on their own, specifically burrows in the ground. The exposure caused his feet to decay so much that they were both amputated with scissors. He described himself an otherwise healthy man when he entered the prison, but left crippled and dying like so many who barely survived.[78]

By August of 1862, just seven months after the camp opened, there were more than 32,000 prisoners taking up an area equipped to house only a small fraction of that number. To accommodate these numbers, the camp was increased to 26.5 acres, though there were approximately 3.25 acres in the center that were so wet and marshy, they were uninhabitable and could not be used in any way.[79] The following photograph of the camp and the various accommodations the prisoners erected prior to the completion of the stockade was taken in August of 1864:

Figure 9. Library of Congress, *Andersonville*. August, 1864, Digital,

450 × 309 pix. Library of Congress, Washington D.C., Available from: DiscerningHistory.com, http://discerninghistory.com (accessed 2 June, 2015).

On the 5th of July, 1864, Confederate Colonel R. H. Chilton was tasked with inspecting the camp and reporting his findings back to Richmond. In a letter to this affect, he described the camp and noted that each prisoner was accommodated less than six square feet of living space—a number that was continually reduced as new men were brought to the camp. He also makes note of the stream running through the camp stating that the cookhouses lie aboveground outside the camp where they use the water to render the food, thus making the water downstream "nearly unfit for use before it reaches the prisoners."[80] This was especially problematic because it essentially meant that none of the 32,000 prisoners had access to clean water for consumption or bathing. Colonel Chilton did mention that the cookhouse was being moved to combat this problem, and also indicated that the prisoners had dug their own wells to find access to potable water throughout the enclosure. Further reports from Confederate officers on the conditions of the camp suggested far worse conditions than Colonel Chilton's account. Confederate Surgeon Joseph Jones called the camp a "gigantic mass of human misery."[81] Assistant Surgeon Thornburgh wrote that the men were completely malnourished, exposed to the harsh sun and heat throughout the day with torrential rain and the morning dew keeping them wet while breathing polluted air and drinking polluted water. He further states that "a pin scratch, a prick of a splinter, an abrasion or even a mosquito bite would cause gangrenous ulcers."[82] The problems were so bad that it became necessary to relocate the camp hospital out of the stockade and to a small grove of trees outside of the walls. This proved to be just as insufficient and fatal due to the overcrowding and complete abundance of prisoners who were sick. Most would die within the first 6-7 months of imprisonment and the weakest were often unable to receive medical care.[83]

During morning sick call, the strongest of the sick would

force their way to the front of the line and be seen first while the weakest men who needed care the most were often unable to make it past their comrades. "The crowd at this these times is so great that only the strongest can get access to the doctors, the weaker ones being unable to force their way through the press."[84] An average of twenty men were carted out of the hospitals each day with most dying of scurvy and chronic diarrhea, primarily due to the complete lack of food. These conditions where no food was provided to the majority of prisoners was somewhat prognosticative of what would happen in the concentration camps of Nazi-occupied Europe and Germany. Pictures of the survivors of Auschwitz and other camps in Nazi-occupied Europe look very similar to those of Andersonville and other Civil War prisons. The below photograph is of a camp survivor who is completely emaciated and malnourished. There is no information as to whether or not this man survived after being released from Andersonville:

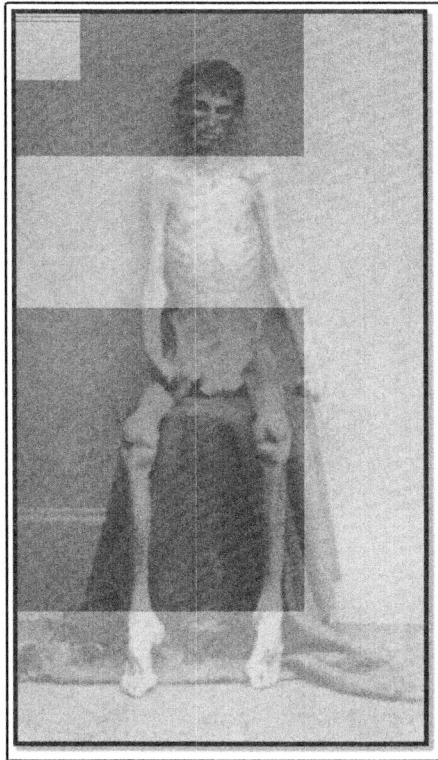

Figure 10. Library of Congress, *Starved Prisoner*. n.d., Digital, 457 × 800 pix. The National Park Service, Washington, D.C. Available from: NPS.gov, http://www.nps.gov/ (accessed 2 June, 2015).

WIRZ AND THE HUMANITARIAN CRISIS IN ANDERSONVILLE

"Several days during the fore part of my imprisonment there we had no rations. The report came from good authority that he was the cause of it, he being in charge of the camp."[85]

Conditions at Andersonville mirrored those of the northern camps in many ways. The local commander, Major Henry Wirz, likely did his best to accommodate the soldiers in his care with little means to do so. While Wirz was the only one to be tried, convicted, and executed of war crimes for what happened at Andersonville, he was an easy scapegoat for blame following the war. Had the Confederacy won and been able to judge the north as harshly as history has judged them and their issues in Andersonville and elsewhere, Wirz would likely have escaped the conflict with his life and dignity. While many were more than willing to come speak out against Major Wirz, former prisoner Second Lieutenant James Madison Page of the Sixth Michigan Cavalry wrote an account of his time in Andersonville and provided a defense of Wirz. Describing his thoughts on Wirz's guilt, Page wrote that "something had to be done to satisfy the popular demand for the punishment of those supposed to be responsible for the suffering and the loss of life among the prisoners, and Major Wirz was doomed, before he was tried, as the party responsible for these results."[86]

Page's account of his time in Andersonville is an excellent repository of information concerning the conditions of the prison and the men who ran it. He offers a surprisingly objective view of Wirz in contrast to his compatriot's accounts depicting the man as the cause for all their suffering. In one instance, he describes a time, shortly after Wirz took command, where the prisoners were allowed a temporary parole to collect fuel (firewood) from the surrounding woods. Several men took advantage of this and fled the area so Wirz was then forced to end this practice. As a result, the men inside the stockade, those Page described as 'the innocent' were left to suffer with no means to cook the food that was provided to them raw. The raw food became an immediate problem for most of his 'Michiganders' as he called them; describing them all as being sick.[87] Because of this, Lieutenant Page requested and was granted an audience with then Captain Wirz to discuss the problems of rations amongst the prisoners. In their exchange, Page notes that Wirz admitted to the problem and that a bakery was being built to alleviate the prisoners' suffering in this respect saying, "There will be a change very soon; the men will soon get bread."[88] This exchange impressed Lieutenant Page such that he commended Wirz in his book and described an increase in rations within just two days of their meeting.

Page's description of the hospitals and surgeons employed there suggest that they too were scapegoats when justice finally came to Andersonville prison. While his account suggests that the men did everything in their limited power to care for the massive amount of injured and infected patients, they were accused in such a way "That they did combine, confederate, and conspire maliciously, traitorously, and in violation of the laws of war, to impair and injure the health and to destroy the lives by subjecting to torture and great suffering" by misplacing personnel amongst the sick and dying to help spread disease.[89] They were also blamed by many for the lack of shelter and exposure to the elements. Page suggests that this is an unfair accusation and that the surgeons, J. H. White, W. J. W. Kerr, and R. R. Stevenson "performed their duty more laboriously or conscientiously than" any other gentleman, north or south.[90]

Further description of the medical personnel and standards of care admit to the overall lack of supplies and beds for the sick. The accusation that the surgeons violated the laws of war suggests an understanding of the common practices of war that existed prior to the First Geneva Convention. Most of the tenets of the First Geneva Convention (Appendix A) describe practices that should have been common but were more an understanding of common decency that standard practice. Prisoners like Lieutenant Page understood this and defended the men who were accused of such violations. His defense is particularly interesting given the seven months he suffered within the confines of Andersonville. Of the surgeons and Wirz, he wrote that thousands of men were in the hospitals and that they were all suffering with thousands dying all the time. He states that the "surgeons in attendance were not more accountable or to blame for it than babes. Neither was Captain Wirz to blame for it."[91] Furthermore, he states that the surgeons as well as Wirz did everything within their power with the means at their disposal to alleviate the suffering of the sick and dying men having acted like "Christians and men."[92]

At his trial, several men came to Wirz's defense like camp surgeon Augustus Moesner who testified that he never heard or saw Captain Wirz injure a Federal prisoner in any way. This was in response to questioning about a prisoner who had allegedly been torn apart by the camp's hounds at Wirz's order. Dr. Moesner insisted that this never happened to his knowledge and similar testimony followed by several people.[93] Though men like Wirz eventually had those like Lieutenant Page come to their defense, there were more than enough to blame him for everything they endured at Andersonville.[94]

George W. Gray of the seventh Indiana Calvary, Company B, testified that he witnessed Wirz shoot a young Private named William Stewart of the 9th Minnesota Infantry. "He and I went out of the stockade with a dead body, and after laying the dead body in the dead-house Captain Wirz rode up to us and asked by what authority we were out there or what we were doing there. Stewart said we were there by proper authority. Wirz said no more, but drew a revolver and shot the man."[95] Such damning testimony was likely only for show as the trial had a foregone conclusion. So many men died at Andersonville and in such horrible conditions that it became necessary for the north and the south to identify someone to take the blame. This fell on the camp's commander and Wirz was eventually hanged for his crimes. He was likely guilty of many things, but may not have been judged so harshly had the circumstances of the war turned out differently for the Confederacy.

Figure 11. National Archives, *Hanging of Cpt. Wirz.* 10 November, 1865, Digital, 700 × 547 pix. The National Archives, Washington, D.C. Available from: NPS.gov, http://www.archives.gov/ (accessed 3 June, 2015).

The humanitarian crisis that became the horror of Andersonville Prison was paramount in the minds of the men who would later bring the United States into the concern of international humanitarian law. After the First Geneva Convention was concluded and the International Committee of the Red Cross was founded, little was done in the embattled states of North America, but once the war was concluded and the two side assessed the horrors that took place on either side, it became apparent that the Lieber Code, the First Geneva Convention, as well as the unwritten laws of war needed to be properly codified and established so that a repeat of the inhumanity of prisoner of war suffering would be repeated in any forthcoming conflict.

THE GENEVA CONVENTIONS AND THE INTERNATIONAL CRIMINAL COURT

"Our species is one, and each of the individuals who compose it is entitled to equal moral consideration. Human rights is the language that systematically embodies this intuition, and to the degree that this intuition gains influence over the conduct of individuals and states, we can say that we are making moral progress."[96]

From agreements on the battlefield to the establishment of the Lieber Code, the most important 'first step' in realizing an international humanitarian rights set of laws and agreements was at the First Geneva Convention, held between the 8th and 22nd of August, 1864. The First Geneva Convention for the Amelioration of the Condition of the Wounded in Armies in the Field was attended by sixteen states, most of which were European monarchs or their representatives. The Convention established principles for the protection of combatants (See Appendix A), which can be summarized into the following three statements:

Relief to the wounded without any distinction as to nationality

Neutrality (inviolability) of medical personnel and medical establishments and units

The distinctive sign of the Red Cross on a white ground[97]

Beyond all other considerations, the First Geneva Convention was meant to address the need to care when it came to injured soldiers as well as the need to protect and identify the aid workers who would endanger themselves in a battlefield while providing care for the wounded. This was paramount in Henri Dunant's concern after the Battle of Solferino and the primary reason for the Convention in the first place. The establishment of the Red Cross as an internationally-recognized symbol of care, aid, and medicine was mean to create a symbol that could be easily recognized by anyone familiar with it.[98] For this reason, it was based off of the Swiss flag, though the colors have been inverted:

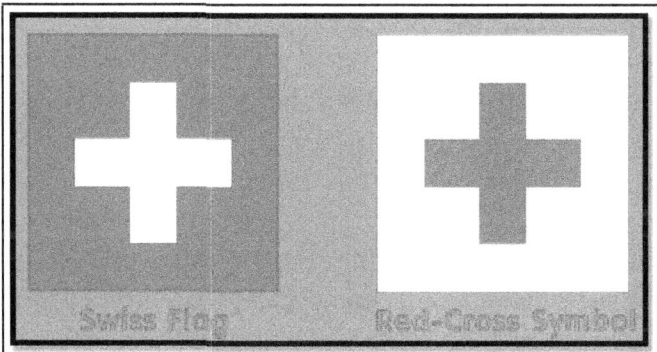

Figure 12. SwitzerlandFacts, *Switzerland Flag – Red Cross Symbol*. n.d., Digital, 1000 x 50 pix. SwitzerlandFacts, Geneva, Switzerland, Available from: SwitzerlandFlag.Facts.co, http:// switzerlandflag.facts.co (accessed 3 June, 2015).

The First Geneva Convention began a process that helped to establish the laws of international human rights throughout the world. Those in attendance who ratified it on the 22nd of August, 1864 were Baden, Belgium, Denmark, France, Hesse, Italy, Netherlands, Portugal, Prussia, Spain, and Switzerland.[99] The United States was also in attendance, though ratification did not occur until the conventions that soon followed.

The second conference to be held took place in October of 1868 for the purpose of clarifying the provisions of the previous convention and to address the need for articles specially addressing naval warfare. The new articles that derived from that meeting were never ratified and thus, never enforced.[100] This would not remain a problem due to the convening of the Hague Convention for the Adaptation to Maritime War of the Principles of the Geneva Convention of August 22, 1864, which was signed at the Hague on the 29th of July, 1899 and aimed to fix the issues of sea warfare and other problems that had arisen since the drafting of the First Geneva Convention articles, which applied only to combat taking place on the ground with no mention of naval warfare.

During the Convention of 1899 and all subsequent meetings concerning the regulations of international humanitarian law, the Lieber Code became a topic of discussion for a number of reasons. Because the Code was very much ahead of its time, it would become superseded by the articles of the Geneva and Hague Conventions that would follow. Regardless of its passages that were considered to be out of date by the late nineteenth century, the Code was often used as a measure for what to do and what not to do. In the United States, the Lieber Code remained a matter of military law until the new Law of War was published by the War Department in 1914, on the eve of World War I.[101] The document opens by saying that "It will be found that everything vital contained in the G.O. 100 [The Lieber Code] ... has been incorporated in this manual."[102] The Lieber Code was in effect as an Army General Order for nearly half-a-century and "Its impact in the United States and internationally was great and long-lasting as the first codification for soldiers in the field of customary rules of battlefield conduct."[103] All subsequent laws of armed conflict that followed such as The Hague Regulations of 1899 and 1907 as well as the Geneva Conventions of 1864 and 1949 all owe a great deal to the Lieber Code of 1863. The Geneva Convention of 1929 expanded on the manner of treatment for those people captured in war by declaring that they must be treated humanely and that the captive nation must supply the names and any other relevant information to the nation of the captured so that arrangements could be made with neutral states to facilitate representation, negotiation, and eventual release. This was detailed in subsequent conventions and was instrumental in determining exactly who was afforded the status of a prisoner of war. One of Lieber's most enduring articles dealt with the treatment of prisoners of war like those kept in the Union and Confederate camps throughout the States at that time.

Lieber makes a distinction between who should be considered a true prisoner of war and who should be considered a "highway robber or pirate."[104] This can be found under Article 82, which indicates that any men who commit a hostile act, but is not a member of any organized military force and who returns to their homes to pretend at 'peaceful pursuits' while pretending to look like soldiers "are not entitled to the privileges of prisoners of war."[105] This is a very important passage because it helped to govern future laws of war such as the Geneva Conventions by determining who could receive prisoner of war status and who could not. The most recent use of this has been the determination made by the United States that the combatants taken from the battlefields in Afghanistan and Iraq during the occupation were unlawful enemy combatants who were not eligible for Geneva Convention regulation or treatment as prisoners of war. On the 7th of February, 2002, President George W. Bush published via the White House Press Secretary that the following:

(1) The 1949 Geneva Convention concerning the treatment of prisoners of war, to which both Afghanistan and the United States are Parties, applies to the armed conflict in Afghanistan between the Taliban and the United States;
(2) That same Convention does not apply to the armed conflict in Afghanistan and elsewhere between al Qaeda and the United States;
(3) Neither captured Taliban personnel nor captured al Qaeda personnel are entitled to be POWs under that Convention; and
(4) Nevertheless, all captured Taliban and al Qaeda personnel are to be treated humanely, consistent with the general principles of the Convention, and delegates of the International Committee of the Red Cross may visit privately

each detainee.[106]

This passage from the White House Press Release has been hotly debated since it was first made public, but even with a great deal of controversy, it does refer back to international law in both the Geneva Convention of 1949 as well as the Lieber Code.

Another article of the Lieber Code that has had a major impact on the development of international humanitarian law was Article 71, which has become the basis for how people are judged under the laws of war. It directly indicates that any personnel who intentionally inflicts injury upon an enemy who is already incapacitated by either causing further harm or by killing them, as well as encouraging or ordering others to do so, will be put to death. It further directs that all members of the United States military would be made aware of this as well as any members of a military force that had been captured by the United States so that they would know their rights.[107] This has probably been the most influential aspect of the Lieber Code on the Geneva Conventions, all of which describe a similar call for anyone who willfully commits a universally-recognized war crime to include genocide and crimes against humanity. While the Lieber Code calls for death in such a case, subsequent agreements have allowed for the creation of an International Criminal Court to determine both guilt and sentencing.

The creation of the International Criminal Court was one of the most far-reaching impacts of the process that began with the Lieber Code. By finally creating an organization that could hold people to account for their actions during wartime, the international body that came to sign the Geneva Conventions finally moved from the period of no accountability to one where anyone who commits an atrocity could eventually be called before a court, tried, an convicted. At present, there are 133 member states that have recognized the jurisdiction of the International Criminal Court and are therefore subject to its oversight. An interesting point of the court and its signatories is that the

United States has yet to ratify its signature on the Rome Statute of the International Criminal Court.[108]

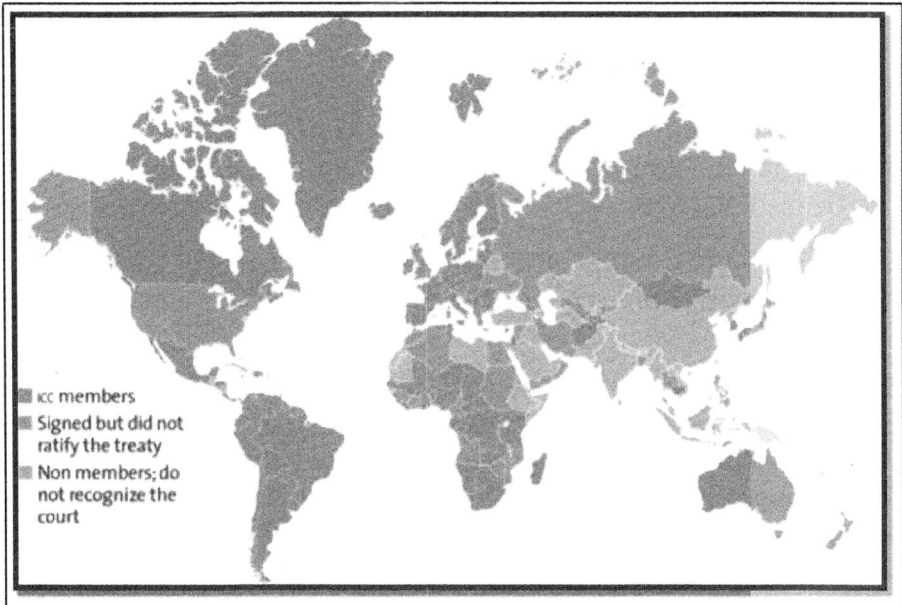

Figure 13. WahalDigital, *Rome Statute of the International Criminal Court*. n.d., Digital, 640 x 417 pix. WahalDigital, Available from: WahalDigital.com, http://wahaldigital.com (accessed 9 June, 2015).

The reasons for this are primarily due to the United States' refusal to allow an international body to try its soldiers and civilians for war crimes. Many in the United States feared that their soldiers might be made example of or prosecuted outside the jurisdiction of the United States, which would possibly violate the United States Constitution's protections on due process, which essentially meant that a Constitutional Amendment might be needed in order to rectify American and International law when dealing with an International Criminal Court. Former Under Secretary of State for Arms Control and International Security, John Bolton, attested to this fact in a letter to former Secretary-General of the United Nations, Mr. Kofi Annan by saying that "the United States does not intend to become a party to the treaty," and that, "[a]ccordingly, the United States has no legal obligations arising from its signature on December 31, 2000."[109] The refusal to ratify the Rome Statute has led to some problems internationally for the United States due primarily to their insistence that American soldiers be immune to the court's jurisdiction. The United States even threatened to remove all of its forces from the ongoing United Nations peacekeeping operations in 2002 if American soldiers were not granted immunity. As a means of compromise, the United Nations Security Council passes a resolution on the

12th of July, 2002, which granted immunity from the Court to any personnel from states that did not ratify the agreement. This was continued for two consecutive twelve month periods until the abuse of Iraqi prisoners of war in Abu Ghraib Prison surfaced at which point the United States dropped its insistence on immunity for its personnel.[110] Despite the United States' objections to the current International Criminal Court and its jurisdiction over its people, the United States of America was one of the most influential states in the establishment of the Court and the conventions that led to its creation. The International Criminal Court can be seen as the ultimate consequence of the Lieber Code and has been used to determine the guilt or innocence of numerous people who have been accused of war crimes to include the mistreatment of prisoners of war.

CONCLUSION

When President Abraham Lincoln decided to push forward with his plans for the emancipation of the slaves in the former Confederate States of America, it is unlikely that he considered his actions would have the far-reaching consequences that they did. Coming from his background as an attorney, he knew that it was necessary to address potential concerns of both his rivals and supporters before engaging in such an incredible act; therefore, he commissioned Francis Lieber to write his famous code.

The Lieber Code was instrumental in changing the manner in which both the United States and subsequent military forces engaged in combat with concern for the laws of war. Being the first code of its kind to be written down and agreed-upon by a government, it established itself as the original document from which all others concerned with the laws of war would eventually follow. Having articles spread throughout it that deal with the treatment of prisoners and the limitations placed on the injury to noncombatants as well as the true requirement for military necessity in combat, no articles were more important than those that addressed the justification for allowing black men to serve in the Union Army. Meant to justify emancipation of former slaves into the United States, it had some far-reaching effects that would not only involve the freeing of the slaves and the introduction of black soldiers into the United States Army, but it would also lead to a severe humanitarian crisis in both the north and the south.

When the Confederate States of America decided that it would not treat captured black soldiers as anything more than criminals or escaped slaves who were to be either returned to a state of servitude or be summarily executed upon capture, all prisoner of war transfers came to an immediate and abrupt halt. It is likely that President Lincoln as well as Francis Lieber did not anticipate such an outcome, which limited their ability to trade black soldiers captured by their enemies, but that was the outcome. The result was an almost-immediate increase in captured personnel not being returned to their home country, which led to a massive influx in the prisoner populations on both sides.

The north and the south had numerous camps erected to deal with the incoming prisoners, but neither was truly prepared for what would come: men by the tens of thousands with little to no food, clothing, supplies, or medicine to sustain them. With both the Confederacy and United States spending most of their money on the ongoing war-effort, neither had much to spare when it came to the humanitarian treatment of their captured prisoners of war. The result was one of the worst humanitarian crisis' to arise in the west since the establishment of the United States of America. Thousands of men died in the harsh and horrible conditions at places like Camp Douglas, Illinois and Andersonville Prison in Georgia.

Though men like Wirz were held to account for their part in the horrific treatment of prisoners in Andersonville, it became apparent to many that more had to be done. While the crisis was ongoing in both the north and the south, Europe was perusing its own solution to similar nightmares. Due to the suffering he witnessed at the Battle of Solferino and the unnecessary lack of care being given to the injured men on the field, Henri Dunant began his own crusade to create a new type of organization that could accommodate the necessary care of injured men in the fields of battle. The result was the creation of the International Committee of the Red Cross in Geneva, Switzerland in 1863. This pursuit resulted in an agency that could potentially deploy personnel anywhere in the world where they might be needed to protect and care for wounded personnel. While the organization had been successfully created and those involved began to petition governments to recognize their right and ability to help, it became apparent that something official needed to be done to bring about an effective change in international law so that the organization could operate without fear of its own demise in and around the battlefields of the world. The result was the calling for an international convention to be held in Geneva in 1864. This became the First Geneva Convention, and it would be attended by numerous countries to include the United States of America, which sent two representatives to observe and return to the United States with their findings.

The First Geneva Convention was held in Geneva in 1864 and can be called a great success in the development of international law regarding humanitarian treatment of personnel wounded in battle. The various articles entered into the Convention and signed by many of the delegates allowed for the autonomy of the International Committee of the Red Cross so that it could operate in harsh conditions without the aid workers fearing for their lives. The most important provisions authorized the creation of an internationally-recognized symbol, the Red Cross, as well as rules stating that any facility so marked would be immune from attack by any side agreeing to the Geneva Convention. Subsequent Geneva Conventions (As well as conventions held at the Hague) would address combat in a naval environment, the treatment of prisoners of war, and even the methods used by militaries in their use of standard and conventional arms, meant to limit further suffering of injured soldiers.

In order for the Geneva Conventions to truly tackle the issues of the laws of war and the treatment of combatants, it was necessary for a continuous review of the Lieber Code since that was the precursor to all of the laws and agreements made in Switzerland in the following one hundred and fifty years. Without the Lieber Code, it is possible that the Geneva Conventions might have halted at only the first one, which would have left a great deal out of international law. Abraham Lincoln's desire to free the slaves had a clear humanitarian goal of not only freeing an entire enslaved populace, but the unintended consequences that came as a result of his ordering the Lieber Code and the Emancipation Proclamation into existence was the development of both the Geneva Conventions and the formal recognition of the International Committee of the Red Cross (And Red Crescent), both of which have been significant events in human history. These events have helped bring humanity out of the dark ages of warfare where little concern was shown to the sick and injured like at the Battle of Solferino or in the stockades of Andersonville. Now that most nations adhere to the principles of the Geneva Conventions and allow for the free movement of members of the International Committee of the Red Cross throughout their lands during conflict, the needless suffering of millions have likely been alleviated and it can all be traced back to President Lincoln, Francis Lieber, and Henri Dunant.

APPENDIX A

The Articles of the First Geneva Convention for the Amelioration of the Condition of the Wounded in Armies in the Field. Geneva, 22 August 1864

Article 1. Ambulances and military hospitals shall be recognized as neutral, and as such, protected and respected by the belligerents as long as they accommodate wounded and sick. Neutrality shall end if the said ambulances or hospitals should be held by a military force.

Art. 2. Hospital and ambulance personnel, including the quartermaster's staff, the medical, administrative and transport services, and the chaplains, shall have the benefit of the same neutrality when on duty, and while there remain any wounded to be brought in or assisted.

Art. 3. The persons designated in the preceding Article may, even after enemy occupation, continue to discharge their functions in the hospital or ambulance with which they serve, or may withdraw to rejoin the units to which they belong. When in these circumstances they cease from their functions, such persons shall be delivered to the enemy outposts by the occupying forces.

Art. 4. The material of military hospitals being subject to the laws of war, the persons attached to such hospitals may take with them, on withdrawing, only the articles which are their own personal property. Ambulances, on the contrary, under similar circumstances, shall retain their equipment.

Art. 5. Inhabitants of the country who bring help to the wounded shall be respected and shall remain free. Generals of the belligerent Powers shall make it their duty to notify the inhabitants of the appeal made to their humanity, and of the neutrality which humane conduct will confer. The presence of any wounded combatant receiving shelter and care in a house shall ensure its protection. An inhabitant who has given shelter to the wounded shall be exempted from billeting and from a portion of such war contributions as may be levied.

Art. 6. Wounded or sick combatants, to whatever nation they may belong, shall be collected and cared for. Commanders-in-Chief may hand over immediately to the enemy outposts enemy combatants wounded during an engagement, when circumstances allow and subject to the agreement of both parties. Those who, after their recovery, are recognized as being unfit for further service, shall be repatriated. The others may likewise be sent back, on condition that they shall not again, for the duration of hostilities, take up arms. Evacuation parties, and the personnel conducting them, shall be considered as being absolutely neutral.

Art. 7. A distinctive and uniform flag shall be adopted for hospitals, ambulances and evacuation parties. It should in all circumstances be accompanied by the national flag. An armlet may also be worn by personnel enjoying neutrality but its issue shall be left to the military authorities. Both flag and armlet shall bear a red cross on a white ground.

Art. 8. The implementing of the present Convention shall be arranged by the Commanders-in-Chief of the belligerent armies following the instructions of their respective Governments and in accordance with the general principles set forth in this Convention.

Art. 9. The High Contracting Parties have agreed to communicate the present Convention with an invitation to accede thereto to Governments unable to appoint Plenipotentiaries to the International Conference at Geneva. The Protocol has accordingly been left open.

Art. 10. The present Convention shall be ratified and the ratifications exchanged at Berne, within the next four months, or sooner if possible.[111]

APPENDIX B

Selections From: INSTRUCTIONS FOR THE GOVERNMENT OF ARMIES OF THE UNITED STATES IN THE FIELD (The Lieber Code, General Order No. 100)

Art. 11. The law of war does not only disclaim all cruelty and bad faith concerning engagements concluded with the enemy during the war, but also the breaking of stipulations solemnly contracted by the belligerents in time of peace, and avowedly intended to remain in force in case of war between the contracting powers.

It disclaims all extortions and other transactions for individual gain; all acts of private revenge, or connivance at such acts.

Offenses to the contrary shall be severely punished, and especially so if committed by officers.

Art. 14. Military necessity, as understood by modern civilized nations, consists in the necessity of those measures which are indispensable for securing the ends of the war, and which are lawful according to the modern law and usages of war.

Art. 15. Military necessity admits of all direct destruction of life or limb of armed enemies, and of other persons whose destruction is incidentally unavoidable in the armed contests of the war; it allows of the capturing of every armed enemy, and every enemy of importance to the hostile government, or of peculiar danger to the captor; it allows of all destruction of property, and obstruction of the ways and channels of traffic, travel, or communication, and of all withholding of sustenance or means of life from the enemy; of the appropriation of whatever an enemy's country affords necessary for the subsistence and safety of the army, and of such deception as does not involve the breaking of good faith either positively pledged, regarding agreements entered into during the war, or supposed by the modern law of war to exist. Men who take up arms against one another in public war do not cease on this account to be moral beings, responsible to one another and to God.

Art. 16. Military necessity does not admit of cruelty - that is, the infliction of suffering for the sake of suffering or for revenge, nor of maiming or wounding except in fight, nor of torture to extort confessions. It does not admit of the use of poison in any way, nor of the wanton devastation of a district. It admits of deception, but disclaims acts of perfidy; and, in general, military necessity does not include any act of hostility which makes the return to peace unnecessarily difficult.

Art. 19. Commanders, whenever admissible, inform the enemy of their intention to bombard a place, so that the noncombatants, and especially the women and children, may be removed before the bombardment commences. But it is no infraction of the common law of war to omit thus to inform the enemy. Surprise may be a necessity.

Art. 21. The citizen or native of a hostile country is thus an enemy, as one of the constituents of the hostile state or nation, and as such is subjected to the hardships of the war.

Art. 22. Nevertheless, as civilization has advanced during the last centuries, so has likewise steadily advanced, especially in war on land, the distinction between the private individual belonging to a hostile country and the hostile country itself, with its men in arms. The principle has been more and more acknowledged that the unarmed citizen is to be spared in person, property, and honor as much as the exigencies of war will admit.

Art. 23. Private citizens are no longer murdered, enslaved, or carried off to distant parts, and the inoffensive individual is as little disturbed in his private relations as the commander of the hostile troops can afford to grant in the overruling demands of a vigorous war.

Art. 35. Classical works of art, libraries, scientific collections, or precious instruments, such as astronomical telescopes, as well as hospitals, must be secured against all avoidable injury, even when they are contained in fortified places whilst besieged or bombarded.

Art. 42. Slavery, complicating and confounding the ideas of property, (that is of a thing,) and of personality, (that is of humanity,) exists according to municipal or local law only. The law of nature and nations has never acknowledged it. The digest of the Roman law enacts the early dictum of the pagan jurist, that "so far as the law of nature is concerned, all men are equal." Fugitives escaping from a country in which they were slaves, villains, or serfs, into another country, have, for centuries past, been held free and acknowledged free by judicial decisions of European countries, even though the municipal law of the country in which the slave had taken refuge acknowledged slavery within its own dominions.

Art. 43. Therefore, in a war between the United States and a belligerent which admits of slavery, if a person held in bondage by that belligerent be captured by or come as a fugitive under the protection of the military forces of the United States, such person is immediately entitled to the rights and privileges of a freeman To return such person into slavery would amount to enslaving a free person, and neither the United States nor any officer under their authority can enslave any human being. Moreover, a person so made free by the law of war is under the shield of the law of nations, and the former owner or State can have, by the law of postliminy, no belligerent lien or claim of service.

Art. 44. All wanton violence committed against persons in the invaded country, all destruction of property not commanded by the authorized officer, all robbery, all pillage or sacking, even after taking a place by main force, all rape, wounding, maiming, or killing of such inhabitants, are prohibited under the penalty of death, or such other severe punishment as may seem adequate for the gravity of the offense.

A soldier, officer or private, in the act of committing such violence, and disobeying a superior ordering him to abstain from it, may be lawfully killed on the spot by such superior.

Art. 47. Crimes punishable by all penal codes, such as arson, murder, maiming, assaults, highway robbery, theft, burglary, fraud, forgery, and rape, if committed by an American soldier in a hostile country against its inhabitants, are not only punishable as at home, but in all cases in which death is not inflicted, the severer punishment shall be preferred.

Art. 49. A prisoner of war is a public enemy armed or attached to the hostile army for active aid, who has fallen into the hands of the captor, either fighting or wounded, on the field or in the hospital, by individual surrender or by capitulation.

All soldiers, of whatever species of arms; all men who belong to the rising en masse of the hostile country; all those who are attached to the army for its efficiency and promote directly the object of the war, except such as are hereinafter provided for; all disabled men or officers on the field or elsewhere, if captured; all enemies who have thrown away their arms and ask for quarter, are prisoners of war, and as such exposed to the inconveniences as well as entitled to the privileges of a prisoner of war.

Art. 53. The enemy's chaplains, officers of the medical staff, apothecaries, hospital nurses and servants, if they fall into the hands of the American Army, are not prisoners of war, unless the commander has reasons to retain them. In this latter case; or if, at their own desire, they are allowed to remain with their captured companions, they are treated as prisoners of war, and may be exchanged if the commander sees fit.

Art. 54. A hostage is a person accepted as a pledge for the fulfillment of an agreement concluded between belligerents during the war, or in consequence of a war. Hostages are rare in the present age.

Art. 55. If a hostage is accepted, he is treated like a prisoner of war, according to rank and condition, as circumstances may admit.

Art. 56. A prisoner of war is subject to no punishment for being a public enemy, nor is any revenge wreaked upon him by the intentional infliction of any suffering, or disgrace, by cruel imprisonment, want of food, by mutilation, death, or any other barbarity.

Art. 57. So soon as a man is armed by a sovereign government and takes the soldier's oath of fidelity, he is a belligerent; his killing, wounding, or other warlike acts are not individual crimes or offenses. No belligerent has a right to declare that enemies of a certain class, color, or condition, when properly organized as soldiers, will not be treated by him as public enemies.

Art. 58. The law of nations knows of no distinction of color, and if an enemy of the United States should enslave and sell any captured persons of their army, it would be a case for the severest retaliation, if not redressed upon complaint.

The United States cannot retaliate by enslavement; therefore death must be the retaliation for this crime against the law of nations.

Art. 59. A prisoner of war remains answerable for his crimes committed against the captor's army or people, committed before he was captured, and for which he has not been punished by his own authorities.

All prisoners of war are liable to the infliction of retaliatory measures.

Art. 63. Troops who fight in the uniform of their enemies, without any plain, striking, and uniform mark of distinction of their own, can expect no quarter.

Art.71. Whoever intentionally inflicts additional wounds on an enemy already wholly disabled, or kills such an enemy, or who orders or encourages soldiers to do so, shall suffer death, if duly convicted, whether he belongs to the Army of the United States, or is an enemy captured after having committed his misdeed.

Art. 74. A prisoner of war, being a public enemy, is the prisoner of the government, and not of the captor. No ransom can be paid by a prisoner of war to his individual captor or to any officer in command. The government alone releases captives, according to rules prescribed by itself.

Art. 75. Prisoners of war are subject to confinement or imprisonment such as may be deemed necessary on account of safety, but they are to be subjected to no other intentional suffering or indignity. The confinement and mode of treating a prisoner may be varied during his captivity according to the demands of safety.

Art. 79. Every captured wounded enemy shall be medically treated, according to the ability of the medical staff.

Art. 105. Exchanges of prisoners take place - number for number - rank for rank wounded for wounded - with added condition for added condition - such, for instance, as not to serve for a certain period.

Art. 106. In exchanging prisoners of war, such numbers of persons of inferior rank may be substituted as an equivalent for one of superior rank as may be agreed upon by cartel, which requires the sanction of the government, or of the commander of the army in the field.

Art. 115. It is customary to designate by certain flags (usually yellow) the hospitals in places which are shelled, so that the besieging enemy may avoid firing on them. The same has been done in battles, when hospitals are situated within the field of the engagement.

Art. 119. Prisoners of war may be released from captivity by exchange, and, under certain circumstances, also by parole.

Art. 120. The term Parole designates the pledge of individual good faith and honor to do, or to omit doing, certain acts after he who gives his parole shall have been dismissed, wholly or partially, from the power of the captor.

Art. 133. No prisoner of war can be forced by the hostile government to parole himself, and no government is obliged to parole prisoners of war, or to parole all captured officers, if it paroles any. As the pledging of the parole is an individual act, so is paroling, on the other hand, an act of choice on the part of the belligerent.[112]

BIBLIOGRAPHY

Primary Sources:

United States War Department. *Rules of Land Warfare.* Washington D.C.: Government Printing Office, 1914.

Bates, Calvin. *Calvin Bates.* April 28, 1865. http://civilwar-talk.com/attachments/34489v-jpg.17823/ (accessed June 2, 2015

Blair, A. G. *A. G. Blair testifying about inhumane treatment.* October 18, 1865. http://law2.umkc.edu/faculty/projects/ftrials/Wirz/xrpt3.htm (accessed June 1, 2015).

Boardman, Mabel Thorp. *Under the Red Cross Flag at Home and Abroad.* Philadelphia: J. B. Lippincott, 1915.

Bolton, John. *Press Statement, International Criminal Court: Letter to UN Secretary General Kofi Annan.* May 9, 2002. http://www.state.gov/r/pa/prs/ps/2002/9968.htm (accessed June 9, 2015).

Bowles, Charles S. P. *Report of Charles SP Bowles foreign agent of the United States sanitary commission upon the International congress of Geneva for the amelioration of the condition of the sick and wounded soldiers of armies in the field convened at Geneva 8th August 1864.* Conference Report, London: Printed by R. Clay, son, and Taylor, 1864.

California. Adjutant General's Office. *Records of California Men in the War of the Rebellion 1861 to 1867.* Sacramento: State Office, 1890.

Chipman, Norton Parker. *The Horrors of Andersonville Rebel Prison: Trial of Henry Wirz, the Andersonville Jailer; Jefferson Davis' Defense of Andersonville Prison Fully Refuted.* San Francisco: Bancroft Company, 1891.

Convention for the Amelioration of the Condition of the Wounded in Armies in the Field. Geneva, 22 August 1864. n.d. https://www.icrc.org/applic/ihl/ihl.nsf/Treaty.xsp?documentId=477CEA122D7B7B3DC12563CD002D6603&action=openDocument (accessed April 28, 2015).

Cooper, S. "General Orders No. 72." *Nih.Gov.* September 29, 1862. http://collections.nlm.nih.gov/pdf/nlm:n-lmuid-101644736-bk (accessed May 26, 2015).

Costa, Dora L., and Matthew E. Kahn. "Surviving Andersonville: The Benefits of Social Networks in POW Camps." *American Economic Review, American Economic Association, vol. 97(4), September,* 2007: 1467-1487.

Davis, Jefferson. *Andersonville and Other War-prisons .* New York: Belford Company, 1890.

Davis, Jefferson, Haskell M. Monroe, James T. McIntosh, and Robert Ould. *The Papers of Jefferson Davis: January-September 1863.* Baton Rouge: Louisiana State University Press, 1971.

Davis, Samuel Boyer. *Escape of a Confederate Officer from Prison: What He Saw at Andersonville. How He was Sentenced to Death and Saved by the Interposition of President Abraham Lincoln.* Norfolk: Landmark Publishing Company, 1892.

Dunant, Henry, and D. H. Wright, trans. *Un Souvenir de Solferino.* Philadelphia: John C. Winston Company, 1911.

Eisenhower, Dwight D. "Executive Order 10631--Code of Conduct for members of the Armed Forces of the United States." *National Archives Federal Register.* August 17, 1955. http://www.archives.gov/federal-register/codification/executive-order/10631.html (accessed April 21, 2015).

Goss, Warren Lee. *The Soldier's Story of His Captivity at Andersonville, Belle Isle, and Other Rebel Prisons .* Boston: L. N. Richardson & Company, 1871.

Gray, George W. *George W. Gray testifying for the prosecution on the charge of murder.* n.d. http://law2.umkc.edu/faculty/projects/ftrials/Wirz/xrpt5.htm (accessed June 3, 2015).

James Brown Scott, ed., trans. *The Proceedings of the Hague Peace Conferences: Plenary meetings of the conference* . Oxford: Oxford University Press, 1920.

Kellogg, Robert H. *Life and Death in Rebel Prisons: Giving a Complete History of the Inhuman and Barbarous Treatment of Our Brave Soldiers by Rebel Authorities, Inflicting Terrible Suffering and Frightful Mortality, Principally at Andersonville, Ga., and Florence, S.C.* Hartford: L. Stebbins, 1867.

Lee, Robert E. "Lee's Famous Orders #72." *ExplorePAHistory.* June 21, 1863. http://explorepahistory.com/kora/files/1/2/1-2-842-25-ExplorePAHistory-a0h4b0-a_349.jpg (accessed May 26, 2015).

Lieber, Francis. *The Lieber Code of 1863.* April 24, 1863. http://www.civilwarhome.com/liebercode.htm (accessed May 2, 2015).

—. "General Orders No. 100 : The Lieber Code." April 24, 1863. http://avalon.law.yale.edu/19th_century/lieber.asp#sec1 (accessed 13 June, 2015).

Lincoln, Abraham. " The Emancipation Proclamation." *Archives.gov.* n.d. http://www.archives.gov/exhibits/featured_documents/emancipation_proclamation/ (accessed May 21, 2015).

—. *June 16, 1858, Address to the Republican Convention.* n.d. http://brotherswar.com/Civil_War_Quotes_4c.htm (accessed May 2, 2015).

Maile, John Levi. *Prison Life in Andersonville.* Los Angeles: Grafton, 1912.

Manual for the Medical Department. Washington D.C.: United States. Army Medical Dept, 1898.

Moesner, Augustus. *Augustus Moesner testifying for the defense on the charge of violating the rules of war.* n.d. http://law2.umkc.edu/faculty/projects/ftrials/Wirz/xrpt4.htm (accessed June 3, 2015).

Page, James Madison, and Michael Joachim Haley. *The True Story of Andersonville Prison: A Defense of Major Henry Wirz.* New

York: Neale Publishing Company, 1908.

Pictet, Jean S. "Commentary on the Geneva Convention Relative to the Treatment of Prisoners of War." *The Geneva Conventions of 12 August 1949.* Geneva: International Committee of the Red Cross, 1949. 1-795.

R. Randolph Stevenson, M.D. *The Southern Side: Or, Andersonville Prison.* Baltimore: Turnbull Brothers, 1876.

Ransom, John L. *Andersonville Diary, Escape, and List of the Dead: With Name, Co., Regiment, Date of Death and No. of Grave in Cemetery.* Auburn: John L. Ransom, 1881.

Seward, William Henry. "United States Department of State / Papers relating to foreign affairs, accompanying the annual message of the president to the second session thirty-eighth congress." *Foreign Relations of the United States.* July 13, 1864. http://digicoll.library.wisc.edu/cgi-bin/FRUS/ FRUS-idx? type=div&did=FRUS.FRUS1864p4.i0014&isize=text (accessed April 28, 2015).

Sperry, C. S. "The Revision of the Geneva Convention, 1906." *Proceedings of the American Political Science Association.* Washington D.C.: American Political Science Association, 1906. 33-57.

Tuttle, Edmund Bostwick. *The History of Camp Douglas: Including Official Report of Gen. B.J. Sweet : with Anecdotes of the Rebel Prisoners.* Chicago: J.R. Walsh, 1865.

United States Government Printing Office. *Congressional Serial Set.* Washington, D.C.: United States Government Printing Office, 1902.

United States Navy Department. *Hague and Geneva Conventions.* Washington D.C.: United States Government Printing Office, 1911.

United States War Department. *Annual Reports of the War Department, Volume 1.* Washington, DC: U.S. Government Printing Office, 1903.

—. *The 1863 Laws of War.* Mechanicsburg: Stackpole Books, 2005.

—. *The war of the rebellion: a compilation of the official records of the*

Union and Confederate armies. ; Series 2 - Volume 7. Washington, D.C.: United States War Department, 1864.

—. *War of the Rebellion: Official Records of the Union and Confederate Armies.* Washington D.C.: Government Printing Office, 1880-1901.

Waide, Susan P., and Valerie Wingfield. *United States Sanitary Commission Records 1861-1878.* Compilation of Records, New York: The New York Public Library, 2006.

Secondary Sources:

A Brief History of the American Red Cross. n.d. http://www.red-cross.org/about-us/history (accessed June 13, 2015).

Abrams, Irwin. *The Nobel Peace Prize and the Laureates: An Illustrated Biographical History, 1901-2001.* Nantucket: Science History Publications/USA, 2001.

Anderson, Chandler P. "The International Red Cross Organization." *The American Journal of International Law Vol. 14, No. 1/2 (Jan. - Apr),* 1920: 210-214.

Bennett, Angela. *The Geneva Convention: The Hidden Origins of the Red Cross.* Gloucestershire: The History Press, 2013 .

Bianchi, Andrea, and Yasmin Naqvi. *Enforcing International Law Norms Against Terrorism.* Portland: Hart Publishing, 2004.

Blackett, R. J. M. *Divided Hearts: Britain and the American Civil War.* Baton Rouge: Louisiana State University Press, 2001.

Bradley, Curtis A. *U.S. Announces Intent Not to Ratify International Criminal Court Treaty.* May 11, 2002. http://www.asil.org/insights/volume/7/issue/7/us-announces-intent-not-ratify-international-criminal-court-treaty (accessed June 9,

2015).

Castel, Albert. "The Fort Pillow Massacre: A Fresh Examination of the Evidence." *Civil War History, Volume 4, Number 1, March,* 1958: 37-50.

Catalano, John. *Francis Lieber: Hermeneutics and Practical Reason.* Lanham: University Press of America, 2000.

Cloyd, Benjamin G. *Haunted by Atrocity: Civil War Prisons in American Memory*. Baton Rouge: Liousiana State University Press, 2010.

Coupland, Robin M. "The effects of weapons and the Solferino cycle ." *British Medical Journal Oct 2; 319,* 1999: 864–865.

Cover, Front. *The Law of Armed Conflict: International Humanitarian Law in War.* Cambridge: Cambridge University Press, 2010.

Davis, Robert Scott. *Andersonville Civil War Prison.* Charleston: The History Press, 2011.

—. *Ghosts and Shadows of Andersonville: Essays on the Secret Social Histories of America's Deadliest Prison.* Macon: Mercer University Press, 2006.

"Declaration by the Presidency on behalf of the European Union on the Occasion of the 150th Anniversary of the Battle of Solferino." *European Union Press Release.* Brussels: The European Union, 2009. 70-71.

Dunkelman, Mark H. *Brothers One and All: Esprit de Corps in a Civil War Regiment.* Baton Rouge: LSU Press, 2004.

Ferrell, Claudine L. *The Abolitionist Movement.* Westport: Greenwood Publishing Group, 2006.

Gillispie, James M. *Andersonvilles of the North: The Myths and Realities of Northern Treatment of Civil War Confederate Prisoners.* Denton: University of North Texas Press, 2008.

Grogg, Mitchell. *Archaeological Dig Underway on South Side - Hope is to dig up parts of Camp Douglas.* June 29, 2012. http://www.nbcchicago.com/news/local/chicago-archae-ological-dig-south-side-civil-war-camp-douglas-160764615.html (accessed June 1, 2015).

Guelzo, Allen C. *Lincoln's Emancipation Proclamation: The End of*

Slavery in America. New York: Simon and Schuster, 2006.

Hall, Yancey. "U.S. Civil War Prison Camps Claimed Thousands." *National Geographic News.* July 1, 2003. http://news.nationalgeographic.com/news/2003/0·/0701_030701_civilwar-prisons.html (accessed April 14, 2015).

Haller, John S. *Battlefield Medicine: A History of the Military Ambulance from the Napoleonic Wars Through World War I.* Carbondale: Southern Illinois University Press, 2011.

Hartigan, Richard Shelly. *Lieber's Code and the Law of War.* Chicago: Transaction Publishers, 1983.

—. *Military Rules, Regulations & the Code of War: Francis Lieber and the Certification of Conflict.* New Brunswick: Transaction Publishers, 2010.

Haye, Eve La. *War Crimes in Internal Armed Conflicts .* Cambridge: Cambridge University Press, 2008.

Helen Durham, Timothy L. H. MacCormack, ed. *The Changing Face of Conflict and the Efficacy of International Humanitarian Law.* The Hague: Martinus Nijhoff Publishers, 1999.

Hesseltine, William Best. *Civil War Prisons.* Kent: Kent State University Press, 1962.

Hillman, Elizabeth L. "Gentlemen Under Fire: The U.S. Military and "Conduct Unbecoming"." *26 Law & Ineq. 1*, 2008: 1-58.

Hudson, Walter M. *Army Diplomacy: American Military Occupation and Foreign Policy After World War II.* Lexington: University Press of Kentucky, 2015.

Hutchinson, John F. *Champions of Charity: War and the Rise of the Red Cross.* Boulder: Westview Press, 1997.

Ignatieff, Michael. *Human Rights as Politics and Idolatry.* Princeton: Princeton University Press, 2001.

Jensen, Richard. *WWW Guide to Civil War Prisons.* April 9, 2004. http://tigger.uic.edu/~rjensen/prisons.htm (accessed June 1, 2015).

Johns, Fleur. "Guantánamo Bay and the." *The European Journal of International Law Vol. 16 no.4*, 2005: 613-635.

Jones, Marian Moser. *The American Red Cross from Clara Barton to the New Deal.* Baltimore: John Hopkins University Press,

2012.

Journey – 150 years of humanitarian action in the midst of armed conflict. August 30, 2013. https://www.icrc.org/eng/re-sources/documents/field-newsletter/2013/india-e-news-letter/journey-08-2013.htm (accessed June 11, 2015).

Kantor, MacKinlay. *Andersonville.* New York: Penguin Group USA, 2015.

Keller, David L. *Story of Camp Douglas: Chicago's Forgotten Civil War Prison, The.* Charleston: Arcadia Publishing, 2015.

Kennedy, David. *Of War and Law.* Princeton: Princeton University Press, 2009.

Kennedy, Robert C. *On This Day, July 12th, 1862.* n.d. https://www.nytimes.com/learning/general/onthisday/harp/0712.html (accessed May 20, 2015).

Kent Masterson Brown, Esq. *Retreat from Gettysburg: Lee, Logistics, and the Pennsylvania Campaign.* Chapel Hill: UNC Press Books, 2005.

Krammer, Arnold. *Prisoners of War: A Reference Handbook.* West-port: Greenwood Publishing Group, 2008.

Laska, Lewis L., and James M. Smith. "Hell and the Devil': Andersonville and the Trial of Captain Henry Wirz, C.S.A., 1865." *Military Law Review, Vol. 68,* 1975: 77-132.

Levy, George. *To Die in Chicago: Confederate Prisoners at Camp Douglas, 1862-65.* Burmaster: Pelican Publishing, 1999.

Lisa Tendrich Frank, ed. *Women in the American Civil War, Volume 1.* Santa Barbara: ABC-CLIO, Inc., 2008.

MacCormack, Timothy L. H., and Helen Durham. *The Changing Face of Conflict and the Efficacy of International Humanitarian Law.* Cambridge: Martinus Nijhoff Publishers, 1999.

Marvel, William. *Andersonville: The Last Depot.* Chapel Hill: University of North Carolina Press, 2006.

McElroy, John. *Andersonville: A Story of Rebel Military Prisons.* Monte Ne: Mundus Publishing, 2011.

McPherson, Dr. James. *A Brief Overview of the American Civil War - A Defining Time In Our Nation's History.* n.d. http://www.civilwar.org/education/history/civil-war-overview/overview.html (accessed June 11, 2015).

McPherson, James M. *Battle Cry of Freedom: The Civil War Era.* Oxford: Oxford University Press, 1988.

Miller, Randall M. *Lincoln and Leadership: Military, Political, and Religious Decision Making.* Bronx: Fordham Univ Press, 2012.

National Park Service. *Locating the Site.* n.d. http://www.nps.gov/nr/twhp/wwwlps/lessons/123 camp_chase/123locate1.htm (accessed May 28, 2015).

Nowlan, Robert A. *The American Presidents, Washington to Tyler: What They Did, What They Said, What Was Said About Them, with Full Source Notes .* Jefferson: McFarland, 2012.

Paust, Jordan J. "Dr. Francis Lieber and the Lieber Code." *Proceedings of the Annual Meeting (American Society of International Law) Vol. 95, (APRIL 4-7),* 2001: 112-115.

Pickenpaugh, Roger. *Camp Chase and the Evolution of Union Prison Policy.* Birmingham: University of Alabama Press, 2007.

—. *Captives in Blue: The Civil War Prisons of the Confederacy.* Tuscaloosa: University of Alabama Press, 2013.

—. "Prisoner Exchange and Parole." *Essential Civil War Curriculum.* May 2012. http://www.essential.civilwar.vt.edu/assets/ files/ECWC%20TOPIC%20Prisoner%20Exchange%20and %20Parole%20Essay2.pdf (accessed May 26, 2015).

Pictet, Jean S. "The New Geneva Conventions for the Protection of War Victims." *The American Journal of International Law Vol. 45, No. 3 (July),* 1951: 462-475.

Pucci, Kelly. *Camp Douglas: Chicago's Civil War Prison.* Charleston: Arcadia Publishing, 2007.

Rome Statute of the International Criminal Court. July 1, 2002. http://www.icc-cpi.int/nr/rdonlyres/ea9aeff7-5752-4f84-be94-0a655eb30e16/0/rome_statute_english.pdf (accessed June 9, 2015).

Rothkopf, Carol Zeman. *Jean Henri Dunant: Father of the Red Cross.* Geneva: Red Cross and Red Crescent, 1969.

Ruhlman, R. Fred. *Captain Henry Wirz and Andersonville Prison: A Reappraisal.* Knoxville: University of Tennessee Press, 2006.

Rutman, Darrett B. "The War Crimes and Trial of Henry Wirz." *Civil War History Volume 6, Number 2, June*, 1960: 117-133.

Sanders, Charles W. *While in the Hands of the Enemy: Military Prisons of the Civil War.* Baton Rouge: Louisiana State University, 2005.

Schindler, Dietrich, and Jiří Toman. *The Laws of Armed Conflicts: A Collection of Conventions, Resolutions, and Other Documents.* Dordrecht: Martinus Nijhoff Publishers, 1988.

Solf, Waldemar A. "Protection of Civilians against the Effects of Hostilities under Customary International Law and under Protocol I." *American University International Law Review*, 1986: 117-137.

Solis, Gary D. *The Law of Armed Conflict: International Humanitarian Law in War.* Cambridge: Cambridge University Press, 2010.

Speer, Lonnie R. *Portals to Hell: Military Prisons of the Civil War.* Mechanicsburg: Stackpole Books, 1997.

Springer, Paul J., and Glenn Robbins. *Transforming Civil War Prisons: Lincoln, Lieber, and the Politics of Captivity.* New York: Routeledge, 2015.

The Election of 1860. n.d. http://www.tulane.edu/~latner/Background/BackgroundElection.html (accessed May 2, 2015).

The ICRC's Mandate and Mission. October 29, 2010. https://www.icrc.org/eng/who-we-are/mandate/overview-icrc-mandate-mission.htm (accessed April 30, 2015).

Toman, Jiří, and Dietrich Schindler. *The Laws of Armed Conflicts: A Collection of Conventions, Resolutions, and Other Documents.* Dordrecht: Martinus Nijhoff Publishers, 1988.

Vansoolen, Louwane. *Fort Douglas.* Charleston: Arcadia Publishing, 2009.

Veuthey, Michael. "Implementation and Enforcement of Humanitarian Law and Human Rights Law in Non-International Armed Conflicts: The Role of the International Committee of the Red Cross." *American University Law Review*, 1983-1984: 83-114.

White, Henry S., and Edward Drewry, ed. Jervey. *Prison Life Among the Rebels: Recollections of a Union Chaplain.* Kent: Kent State University Press, 1990.

Witt, John Fabian. *Lincoln's Code: The Laws of War in American History.* New York: Simon and Schuster, 2013.

Lincoln's Code: The Laws of War in American History. Directed by Duke Law School. Performed by Professor John Fabian Witt. 2012.

Glory. Directed by Edward Zwick. 1989.

---

[1] Poleis were city-states in ancient Greece. The two largest and most powerful poleis were Athens and Sparta. They functionally acted as independent countries with cultural affiliations with one another. They would eventually come together and form the nation of Greece, but were initially separate and often battled one another.

[2] Mabel Thorp Boardman, *Under the Red Cross Flag at Home and Abroad* (Philadelphia: J. B. Lippincott, 1915), 24.

[3] Robert A. Nowlan, *The American Presidents, Washington to Tyler: What They Did, What They Said, What Was Said About Them, with Full Source Notes* (Jefferson: McFarland, 2012), 43.

[4] The Battle of Solferino was the largest battle during the Second Italian War of Independence fought between the armies of France and Sardinia against Austria. There were more than 300,000 combatants with a high number of wounded and killed on both sides. Dunant toured the aftermath of the battle and saw the lack of medical treatment for the wounded, leaving most to die on the battlefield.

[5] "Declaration by the Presidency on behalf of the European Union on the Occasion of the 150th Anniversary of the Battle of Solferino," *European Union Press Release.* Brussels: The European Union, 2009. 70.

[6] Clara Barton was a prominent nurse who served in numerous battled and ended the war with the governance of all military hospitals. After the American Civil War, she would travel to Geneva and become a major player in establishing the American Red Cross. She is recognized as an important historical figure who was nicknamed "The Angel of the Battlefield" for her work during the war.

[7] The United States Sanitary Commission was a private organization established in the North to provide relief to the sick and wounded Soldiers of the Union Army. It was modeled off of the British Sanitary Commission, which was established during the Crimean War. In many ways, it was the precursor to the International Committee of the Red Cross.

[8] William Henry Seward, "United States Department of State / Papers relating to foreign affairs, accompanying the annual message of the president to the second session thirty-eighth congress," *Foreign Relations of the United States,* July 13, 1864, http://digicoll.library.wisc.edu/cgi-bin/FRUS/FRUS-idx?type=div&did=FRUS.FRUS1864p4.i0014&isize=text (accessed April 28, 2015).

[9] Angela Bennett, *The Geneva Convention: The Hidden Origins of the Red Cross* (Gloucestershire: The History Press, 2013), 19.

[10] Carol Zeman Rothkopf, *Jean Henri Dunant: Father of the Red Cross* (Geneva: Red Cross and Red Crescent, 1969.), 126.

[11] John F. Hutchinson, *Champions of Charity: War and the Rise of the Red Cross* (Boulder: Westview Press, 1997), 11.

[12] Gary D. Solis, *The Law of Armed Conflict: International Humanitarian Law in War* (Cambridge: Cambridge University Press, 2010), 38-44.

[13] Nearly all scholarship is certain that slavery was the cause of the Civil War though many still argue it to this day. The best explanation of what brought about the Civil War was described by McPherson where he wrote "The Civil War started because of uncompromising differences between the free and slave states over the power of the national government to prohibit slavery in the territories that had not yet become states. When Abraham Lincoln won election in 1860 as the first Republican president on a platform pledging to keep slavery out of the territories, seven slave states in the deep South seceded and formed a new nation, the Confederate States of America. The incoming Lincoln administration and most of the Northern people refused to recognize the legitimacy of secession. They feared that it would discredit democracy and create a fatal precedent that would eventually fragment the no-longer United States into several small, squabbling countries." Dr. James McPherson, "A Brief Overview of the American Civil War - A Defining Time In Our Nation's History," n.d., http://www.civilwar.org/education/history/civil-war-overview/overview.html (accessed 11 June, 2015).

[14] Robert Scott Davis, *Andersonville Civil War Prison* (Charleston: The History Press, 2010), 113.

[15] Kelly Pucci, Camp Douglas: Chicago's Civil War Prison (Charleston: Arcadia Publishing, 2007), 108.

[16] Paul J. Springer and Glenn Robins, *Transforming Civil War Prisons: Lincoln, Lieber, and the Politics of Captivity* (New York: Routledge, 2014), 9.

[17] David H. Wright, Mrs., *The Origin of the Red Cross* (Philadelphia: John C. Winston Company, 1911), viii.

[18] Calvinism is a major branch of Protestantism, which was predominantly influenced by John Calvin.

[19] The Young Men's Christian Association (YMCA) was founded in London in 1844 yet maintains its current headquarters in Geneva, Switzerland where Jean-Henri Dunant founded a chapter in 1852.

[20] Abrams, 47.

[21] Harriet Beecher Stowe as an American author and abolitionist who wrote the novel, *Uncle Tom's Cabin*, in 1852. Her work was instigative of the abolitionist movement and helped to further the cause for the abolishment of slavery in the United States and abroad. She wrote more than twenty books during her lifetime and is remembered as one of the most influential women of the later nineteenth century in American culture.

[22] Abrams, 47.

[23] "History of Red Cross," *Austrian Red Cross*. n.d. http://www.roteskreuz.at/fileadmin/user_upload/PDF/Austrian_Red_Cross/RC_History.pdf (accessed April 30, 2015).

[24] The Second Italian War of Independence was fought between April 29th, to July 11th, 1859 between the French, Sardinians, and Austrians. It is also known as the Franco-Austrian and/or Austro-Sardinian War. It was instrumental in the unification of Italy; a process that had been ongoing since 1815 and would not be finalized until 1871.

[25] Wright, 4.

[26] *Ibid.,* 5.

[27] *Ibid.,* 15.

[28] *Ibid..* 17.

[29] Wright,. 71.

[30] ICRC is the acronym for International Committee of the Red Cross (Also Red Crescent).

[31] Wright, 78.

[32] The ICRC's Mandate and Mission, October 29, 2010, https://www.icrc.org/eng/who-we-are/mandate/overview-icrc-mandate-mission.htm (accessed April 30, 2015).

[33] The Geneva Society for Public Unity was formed in 1828 with the goal of bringing together "Men of affairs who sought to improve both the moral and the material lives of the common people." (Hutchinson, 21.)

[34] John F. Hutchinson, *Champions of Charity: War and the Rise of the Red Cross* (Boulder: Westview Press, Inc., 1997), 11.

[35] Hutchinson, 23.

[36] The Sonderbund War of 1847 was civil war in Switzerland that lasted from 3-29 November and brought about the end of the newly constituted Sonderbund. The result was the federal constitution of Switzerland in 1848.

[37] Hutchinson, 22-23.

[38] *Ibid.,* 24.

[39] The American Red Cross was founded by Clara Barton and some close acquaintances in Washington, D.C. on the 21st of May, 1881. Barton was first

introduced to the organization when she visited Geneva following the Civil War. She became inspired to create a similar organization in the United States and she also began a campaign to get the United States to ratify the First Geneva Convention to ensure the newly-formed American Red Cross would be recognized in the same noncombatant role as the International Committee of the Red Cross throughout Europe. "A Brief History of the American Red Cross," n.d., http://www.redcross.org/about-us/history (accessed 13 June, 2015).

[40] John Catalano, *Francis Lieber: Hermeneutics and Practical Reason* (Lanham: University Press of America, 2000), 9.

[41] This was especially true in the late Roman Republic during several servile insurrections. One of the most famous was the Third Servile War (73-71 B.C.E.), which gave rise to the story of Spartacus. That war saw the insurrection of more than 120,000 former slaves who turned on their masters. A more recent conflict that was likely on the minds of the Southern whites was the uprising of Saint-Domingue, where the local slave population rose against their French masters and eventually drove them off the island in 1803. The Republic of Haiti was then declared an independent state in 1804.

[42] R. J. M. Blackett, *Divided Hearts: Britain and the American Civil War* (Baton Rouge: Louisiana State University Press, 2001), 29.

[43] One of Lieber's sons, Oscar Montgomery Lieber, joined the war on the side of the Confederacy and was killed at the Battle of Eltham's Landing in May of 1862. Adversely, his other two sons, Guido Norman and Hamilton Lieber both joined the Union Army and fought for their respective sides.

[44] Francis Lieber, "The Lieber Code of 1863," April 24th, 1863, Article 15, http://www.civilwarhome.com/liebercode.htm (accessed 2 May, 2015).

[45] Lieber, Articles 42-43.

[46] Abraham Lincoln, "The Emancipation Proclamation," *Archives.gov*, n.d., http://www.archives.gov/exhibits/featured_documents/emancipation_proclamation/ (accessed 21 May, 2015).

[47] Lieber, Article 49.

[48] Robert C. Kennedy, "On this Day, July 12th, 1862," https://www.nytimes.com/learning/general/onthisday/harp/0712.html (accessed 20 May, 2015).

[49] Davis General Order 111

[50] *Ibid.*

[51] Albert Castel, The Fort Pillow Massacre: A Fresh Examination of the Evidence, *Civil War History Volume 4, Number 1, March* (1958), 47.

[52] This was depicted in the film, *Glory*, which had a scene where the commanding officer of a Black Union Army Regiment, the Massachusetts 54th, read General Davis' order (A film version of it) to his gathered regiment. Offering to release any men from their oaths of enlistment or commission (Extended to the white officers of the unit), the Colonel expected most of his men to be gone by the next morning's muster. When he awoke the next day, he found that not a

single man had left the unit. *Glory*. Directed by Edward Zwick. Beverly Hills: Freddie Fields Productions, 1989.

[53] WM. H. Ludlow, *Congressional Serial Set* (Washington, D.C.: United Sates Government Printing Office, 1902), 18.

[54] The word furlough means a leave of absence and has since been replaced in regular speech as simply 'leave' within the military.

[55] Roger Pickenpaugh, ""

[56] United States War Department, *War of the Rebellion: Official Records of the Union and Confederate Armies* (Washington: Government Printing Office, 1880-1901), Series II, volume 1, 504-505.

[57] Philip Shaw Paludan, *The Presidency of Abraham Lincoln* (Lawrence: University of Kansas Press, 1994), 53.

[58] United States War Department, 267.

[59] Robert Ould was an attorney who worked for the Confederacy during the Civil War. When he was given the task of overseeing prisoner exchanges, he was commissioned in the rank of Colonel, which he held until the end of the war.

[60] General Order 72

[61] Robert Ould, *The Papers of Jefferson Davis: January-September 1863* (Baton Rouge: Louisiana State University Press, 1971), 106.

[62] *Ibid.*

[63] The Confederacy refused to recognize that any blacks were considered to be free men and would place them back into a presumptive state of enslavement regardless of their prior status.

[64] WM. H. Ludlow, *Congressional Serial Set* (Washington, D.C.: United Sates Government Printing Office, 1902), 18.

[65] George Levy, *To Die in Chicago: Confederate Prisoners at Camp Douglas, 1862-65* (Burmaster: Pelican Publishing Company, Inc., 1999), bc.

[66] National Park Service, "Locating the Site" http://www.nps.gov/nr/twhp/wwwlps/lessons/123camp_chase/123locate1.htm (accessed 28 May, 2015).

[67] Roger Pickenpaugh, *Camp Chase and the Evolution of Union Prison Policy* (Birmingham: University of Alabama Press, 2007), 121.

[68] Roger Pickenpaugh, *Camp Chase and the Evolution of Union Prison Policy* (Birmingham: University of Alabama Press, 2007), 121.

[69] Levy, 41.

[70] Henry W. Bellows, http://ehistory.osu.edu/books/official-records/117/0106 (accessed 28 May, 2015).

[71] Henry W. Bellows, http://ehistory.osu.edu/books/official-records/117/0106 (accessed 28 May, 2015).

[72] Levy, 85.

[73] *Ibid.*, 106.

[74] *Ibid.*, 118.

[75] *Ibid.*, 124.

[76] *Ibid.*

[77] John L. Ransom, "Andersonville," n.d., http://www.civilwar.org/education/history/warfare-and-logistics/warfare/famous-quotes-for-andersonville-page.html?referrer=https://www.google.de/ (accessed 1 June, 2015).

[78] Calvin Bates, "Calvin Bates," http://civilwartalk.com/attachments/34489v-jpg.17823/
(accessed 2 June, 2015).

[79] United States War Department, *The war of the rebellion: a compilation of the official records of the Union and Confederate armies. ; Series 2 - Volume 7* (Washington D.C.: United States War Department, 1864), 546.

[80] United States War Department, *The war of the rebellion: a compilation of the official records of the Union and Confederate armies. ; Series 2 - Volume 7* (Washington D.C.: United States War Department, 1864), 546.

[81] James Ford Rhodes, *History of the United States from the Compromise of 1850 to the Final Restoration of Home Rule at the South in 1877: 1864-1866* (London: Macmillan, 1912), 494.

[82] *Ibid.*

[83] *Ibid.*

[84] United States War Department, *The war of the rebellion: a compilation of the official records of the Union and Confederate armies. ; Series 2 - Volume 7* (Washington D.C.: United States War Department, 1864), 547.

[85] A. G. Blair, "A. G. Blair testifying about inhumane treatment," 23 August-18 October, 1865, http://law2.umkc.edu/faculty/projects/ftrials/Wirz/xrpt3.htm (accessed 2 June, 2015).

[86] James Madison Page and Michael Joachim Haley, *The True Story of Andersonville Prison: A Defense of Major Henry Wirz* (New York: Neale, 1908), 11.

[87] Page & Haley, 78.

[88] *Ibid.*, 79.

[89] *Ibid.*, 81-82.

[90] *Ibid.*, 81.

[91] Page & Haley, 83.

[92] *Ibid.*

[93] Augustus Moesner, "Augustus Moesner testifying for the defense on the charge of violating the rules of war," http://law2.umkc.edu/faculty/projects/ftrials/Wirz/xrpt4.htm (accessed 2 June, 2015).

[94] Page's book was not written until 1909, more than thirty years after Wirz was hanged. He explains this in his introduction as his guilt overcoming him after a time and his need to write down what he felt was important in a way to clear his conscience.

[95] George W. Gray, "George W. Gray testifying for the prosecution on the charge of murder," http://law2.umkc.edu/faculty/projects/ftrials/Wirz/xrpt5.htm (accessed 3 June, 2015).

[96] Michael Ignatieff, *Human Rights as Politics and Idolatry* (Princeton: Princeton University Press, 2001), 3-4.

[97] Dietrich Schindler and Jiří Toman, ed., *The Laws of Armed Conflicts: A Collection of Conventions, Resolutions, and Other Documents* (Dordrecht: Martinus Nijhoff Publishers. 1988), 36.

[98] The Swiss flag's design was also chosen because the Convention was held in Geneva and it was meant to pay homage to Dunant and the members of the Committee who organized the First Geneva Convention.

[99] Bavaria, Hesse, and Baden are all territories in Germany. Bavaria and Hesse are both states in modern Germany while Baden comprises several territories into the state of Baden-Württemberg.

[100] Even though the agreement never went into force, the parties involved in the Franco-German War of (1870-1871) and the Spanish-American War of 1898 unofficially agreed to adhere to the principles agreed upon in 1868.

[101] Gary D. Solis, *The Law of Armed Conflict: International Humanitarian Law in War* (Cambridge: Cambridge University Press, 2010), 46.

[102] United States War Department, *Rules of Land Warfare* (Washington D.C.: Government Printing Office, 1914), 7.

[103] Solis., 46.

[104] Lieber (Article 82)

[105] *Ibid.*

[106] Andrea Bianchi and Yasmin Naqvi, *Enforcing International Law Norms Against Terrorism* (Portland: Hart Publishing, 2004), 41.

[107] Lieber Article 71

[108] The Rome Statute of the International Criminal Court, 17 July, 1998, is a statute of the court that entered into force on the 1st of July, 2002. It was signed by 133 countries, though not ratified by all of them. It is an agreement by all signing bodies that the International Criminal Court has jurisdiction over their citizens in the matter of war crimes, genocide, and crimes against humanity. "Rome Statute of the International Criminal Court," 1 July, 2002, http://www.icc-cpi.int/nr/rdonlyres/ea9aeff7-5752-4f84-be94-0a655eb30e16/0/rome_statute_english.pdf (accessed 9 June, 2015).

[109] John Bolton, "Press Statement, International Criminal Court: Letter to UN Secretary General Kofi Annan," 6 May, 2002, http://www.state.gov/r/pa/prs/

ps/2002/9968.htm (accessed 9 June, 2015).

[110] "Q&A: International Criminal Court," 11 March, 2013, http://www.bbc.co.uk/news/world-11809908 (accessed 9 June, 2015).

[111] "Convention for the Amelioration of the Condition of the Wounded in Armies in the Field. Geneva, 22 August 1864," https://www.icrc.org/ihl/INTRO/120?OpenDocument (accessed 12 May, 2015).

[112] Francis Lieber, "General Orders No. 100 : The Lieber Code," 24 April, 1863, http://avalon.law.yale.edu/19th_century/lieber.asp#sec1 (accessed 13 June, 2015).

Printed in Great Britain
by Amazon

22329282R00057